DH MOSQUITO BOMBERS

Part One. Single Stage Merlin Variants

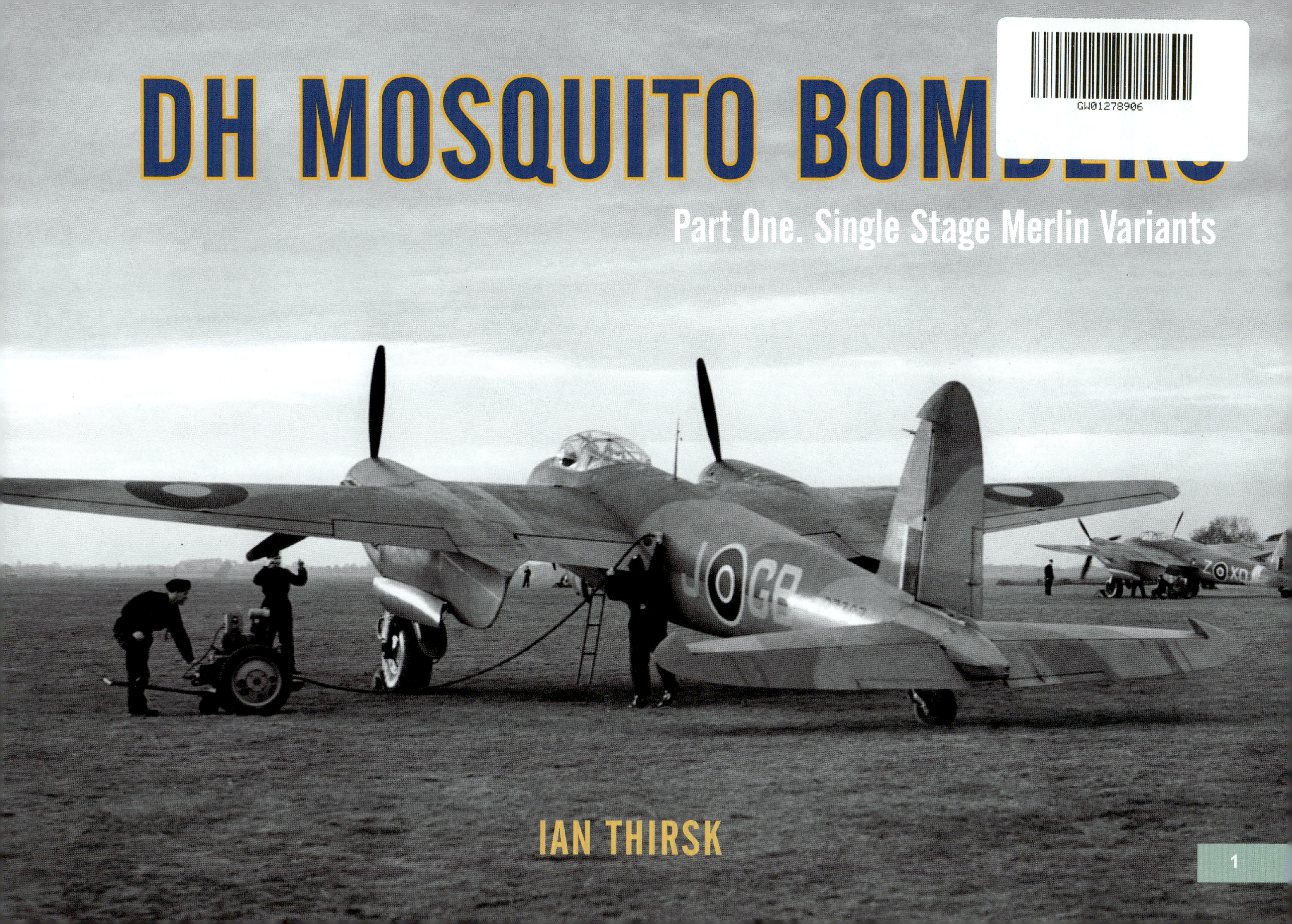

IAN THIRSK

ORIGINS

Below: The prototype Mosquito nearing completion at de Havilland's Salisbury Hall facility in October 1940. Close to Hatfield, the manor house of Salisbury Hall provided peace and security for the design team, construction of the prototype taking place in a hangar disguised as a barn. The fabric covered elevators and rudder appear to be finished in red dope with the remainder of the airframe possibly in a light coat of silver. The rectangular opening behind the canopy housed the dinghy box. The detailed mock-up is visible far right.

Above right: Note the Handley Page leading edge slats (A) on the port wing, shown here in the closed position. Unique to the prototype, these were not incorporated on production aircraft as stall behaviour deemed them unnecessary. On 3 November 1940, the dismantled prototype was transported to Hatfield for flight testing.

Right: The reassembled prototype following 'roll out' at Hatfield, by now finished in trainer yellow with black spinners. Note the ducted exhaust (A) with its outlet curved to exit through the engine side cowling. Located beneath the starboard wing (mirrored on the port side) is what appears to be a fuel jettison pipe (B), another feature unique to the prototype. Undercarriage doors have still to be installed.

Above: Close-up of the starboard inner exhaust ducting angled to eject beneath the wing (C). Note the close proximity of the leading-edge radiator housing, the exhaust exiting directly beneath the oil cooler section of the radiator matrix.

Above right: The prototype being prepared for initial engine runs. It wears the Class B registration 'E0234' denoting a prototype aircraft without a full certificate of airworthiness ('E' being the prefix letter allotted to de Havilland's). Note the 'tear drop' shaped observation blisters on the canopy side panels. EO234 wears 'type A' fuselage roundels and fin flashes, type B' roundels being visible on the wing upper surfaces.

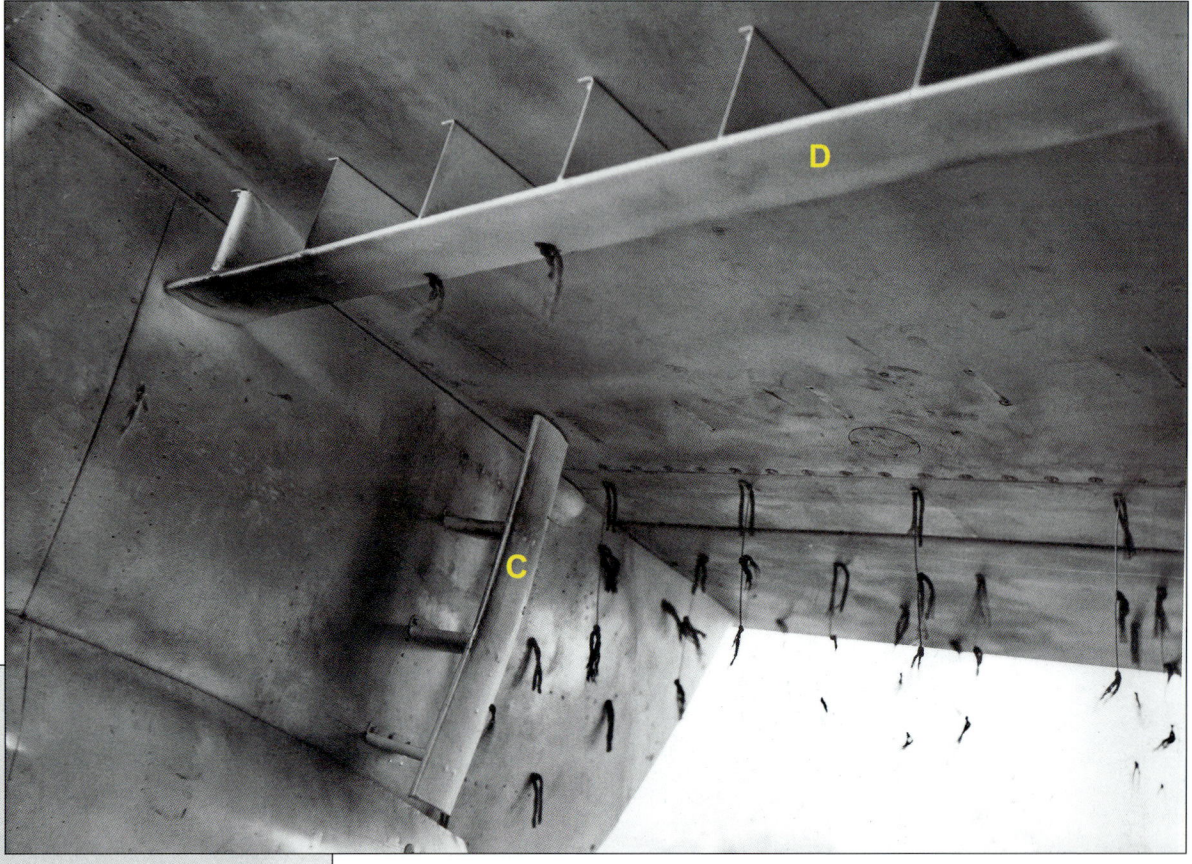

Left: EO234's tail is held down as the port Merlin 21 bursts into life. The line of dashes (A) between the spinner and wing leading edge are Dzus fasteners connecting the side and top cowling panels. Note the 'type A' underwing roundel.

Above left: EO234 prior to the first taxying trials on 24 November 1940. The prototype had a wingspan of 52ft 5in compared to 54ft 2in on production aircraft, the shorter wingtips (B) markedly evident here. By 10 January 1941 the Air Ministry serial 'W4050' had replaced 'EO234'.

Inset above: Aerodynamic 'slots' fitted to W4050's starboard inner nacelle (C) and underwing (D) in an attempt to cure tail buffeting. Above 240 mph a stall was taking place along the inner nacelle and underwing, the disturbed airflow striking the tailplane and causing the airframe to vibrate throughout. Several 'slot' configurations were tested (this one on 10 January 1941) and while buffeting was reduced, they did not eliminate the problem.

EXTENDED NACELLES

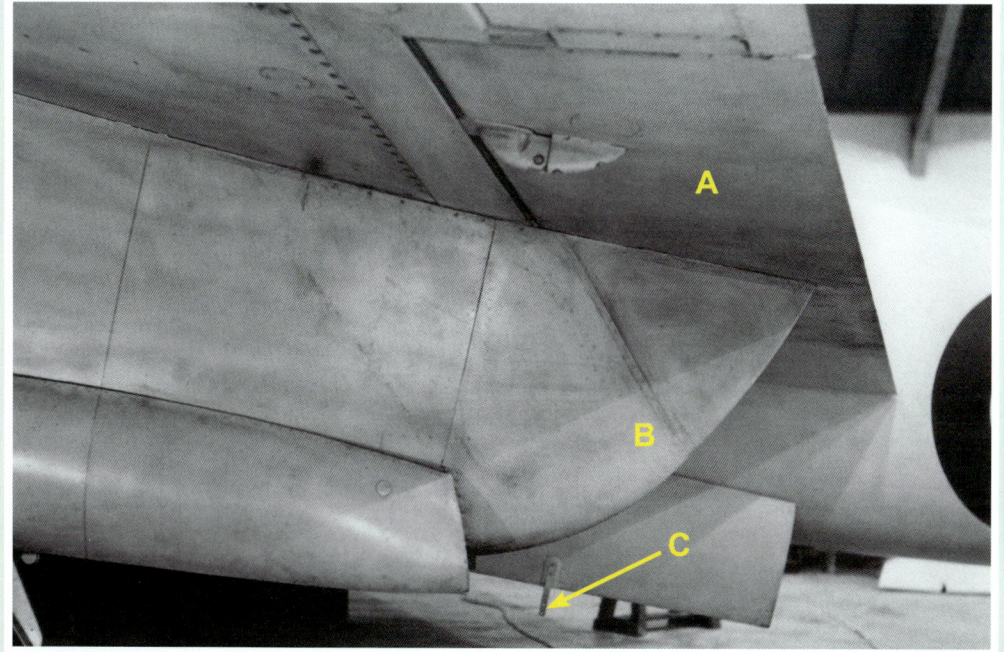

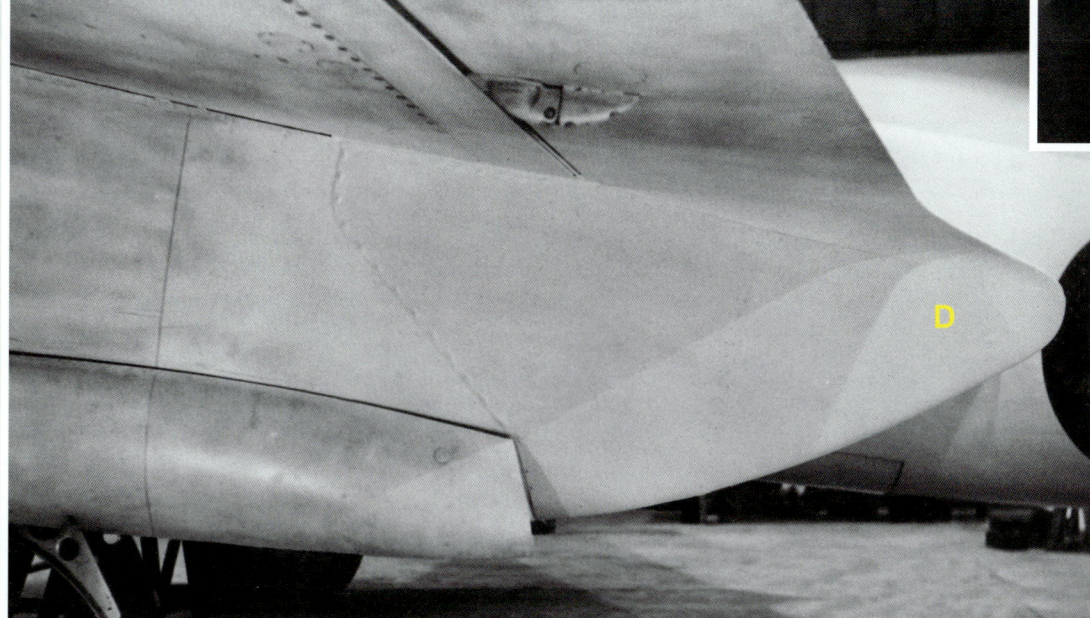

Above left: W4050's port undercarriage nacelle illustrating the original 'short' configuration, the one-piece flap (A) retracting into the nacelle's lower section (B). W4050 did not feature hydraulically operated bomb doors, hence the manual locking strap (C).

Left: RAE Farnborough recommended lengthening the undercarriage nacelles to resolve the tail buffeting. Wind tunnel models showed improved air separation from the rear sections by extending them aft of the wing. This illustrates the first stage of lengthening consisting of faired-in triangular plates (D). Test flown on 3 February 1941; the plates made little difference to handling but reduced turbulence.

Above right: W4050's second (E) and third (F) nacelle extensions. Test flown on 9 February 1941, these were reported as having the 'greatest curative effect of tail buffet to date', wool tufts indicating far less turbulence away from the nacelles. The production shape extension (initially flown on Fighter prototype W4052) was achieved by lengthening the lower fairing (F) until it met the point of the fillet (E). This resulted in the most visible alteration to the original airframe design.

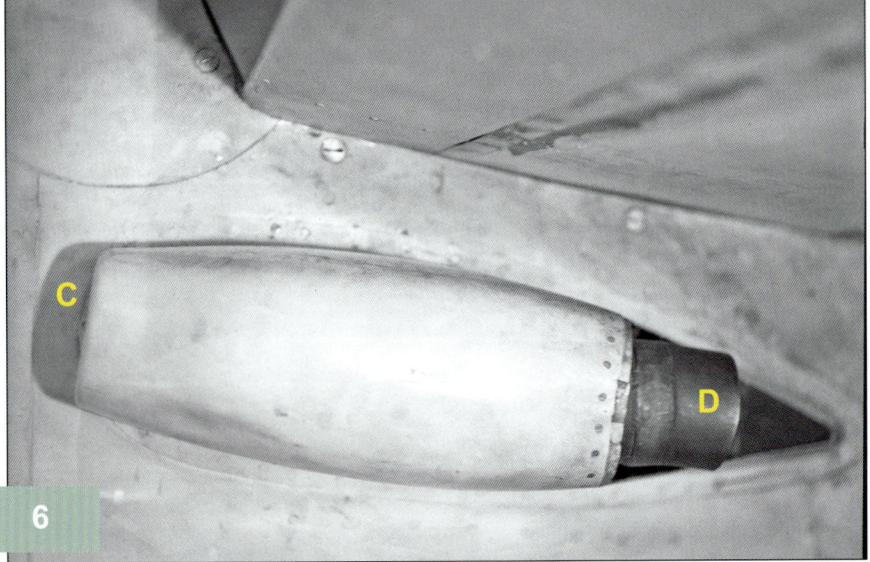

Above left: An aerodynamic fillet (A) positioned directly above the starboard inner exhaust fairing on W4050. Tested in conjunction with aerodynamic slots the fillet was designed to reduce tail buffeting but proved ineffective. The intake (B) on the side cowling was added to address on-going cooling problems with the complex exhaust ducting system.

Left: The starboard inner exhaust fairing on W4050 showing the cooling intake (C) at the forward section and the ejector nozzle (D) at the rear. Overheating issues with this ducted exhaust system - including engine fires and blistered cowlings - led to its replacement by 'saxophone' flame damping shrouds or individual exhaust stubs (see P.42 & 43)

Above right: The starboard main undercarriage of W4050 photographed in May 1941. Note the 'hoop' shape (E) connecting the undercarriage leg fenders across the mainwheel tyre. As the undercarriage was lowered the fenders pushed open the undercarriage doors by engaging with Bakelite rubbing strips on the door inner faces. A feature of the initial prototypes only, the 'hoop' fender was modified for production aircraft by removing the centre piece and adding a support strut from each undercarriage leg. Protruding from the forward fuselage is the trailing aerial tube (F).

Main photo: Photographs of W4050 airborne are extremely rare, this one dates from summer 1941 by which time the upper surfaces were refinished in the standard prototype colours of Dark Earth and Dark Green disruptive camouflage (the demarcation extending as a wavy line down the engine side cowlings) with the under surfaces remaining Trainer Yellow. The fuselage 'Circle P' marking has its lower half outlined in black, the serial number being applied in yellow. Still equipped with Merlin 21's, W4050 also retains the original 'short' undercarriage nacelles.

Inset: W4050 during a display of new aircraft types held at Hatfield in April 1941, the '5' on the rudder denoting it as fifth in the programme. Appearing much as it did the previous November, W4050's fuselage had been replaced (with that from photo-reconnaissance prototype W4051) the previous month following an incident during trials at A&AEE Boscombe Down. This raises an interesting question as prior to A&AEE trials, W4050's upper surfaces were reportedly repainted in Dark Earth and Dark Green camouflage, but the replacement fuselage is clearly yellow in this photo, as is the fin and rudder. The manifold cooling intake on the engine side cowling has been lengthened and the canopy 'tear drop' observation blisters replaced by flat panels.

DAY BOMBERS B.IV SERIES I

Main photo: W4057, the Mosquito bomber prototype, photographed at Hatfield on 5 September 1941. Equipped with the strengthened or 'basic' wing of the projected B. V, W4057 also served as prototype for the first bomber variant, the B.IV Series I. The colour scheme is trainer yellow under-surfaces and Dark Earth/Dark Green upper camouflage. The red, white, blue, and yellow fuselage roundel is 42 inches diameter and the red, white, and blue fin flash 27 inches high by 24 inches wide. The 'Circle P' prototype marking is in yellow and the serial number in black, as are the spinners. Of note is the aerial mast plus the unpainted top frame (A) of the dinghy box, visible immediately aft of the canopy. The 'basic' wing tested on W4057 incorporated underwing hard points for the carriage of bombs, being introduced on the bomber production line with the B. IX.

Inset: The original form of wing tip fitted to Mosquito bombers. Detachable units, wing tips were constructed of plywood outer skin attached to spruce formers and a laminated spruce edge. This is the underside of a starboard wing tip and features navigation (B) and formation keeping (C) lamps built into the tip edge, both within clear perspex covers. For attachment to the wing, screws inserted through Bakelite-reinforced strips (D) on the tip edges, engaged with anchor nuts on the main wing structure. Note the lamp inspection doors (E & F), both secured by Dzus fasteners.

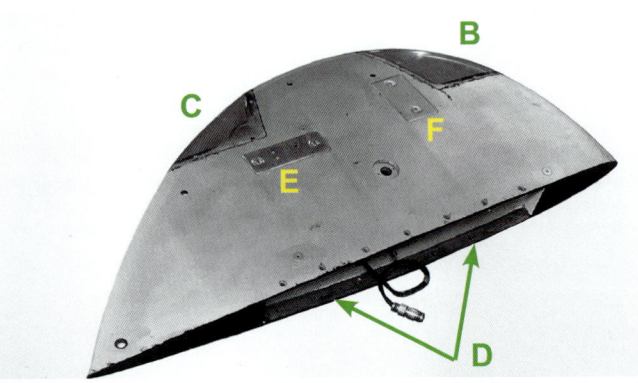

(Production of B.IV Series I Mosquitoes underway at Hatfield in 1941).

Upper left: The port fuselage half-shell of W4070 suspended in its vertical cradle during fitting out. W4070's construction number '98021' is clearly visible on the cradle's forward section (A).

Lower left: Fuselage half shells mated in their 'boxing up' fixture and cramped together using wooden bands with turnbuckle fasteners (B).

Upper right: With its fuselage assembled to the wing, factory workers adjust the throttle and pitch control torque tubes (C) mounted along the front spar.

Below: This shows to advantage the wing's single piece flap design (D) together with the opening (E) for the flap jack access panels on the trailing edge.

Main photo: W4064, the first of nine production B.IV Series I's, at Hatfield following demonstration to the de Havilland workforce in November 1941. A conversion of the PR. I airframe (referred to by de Havilland's as 'PRU/Bomber Conversions'), they retained the latter's 'short' undercarriage nacelles, ducted exhaust system and 19ft 5.5-inch span 'No.1 tailplane'. Finished in the Temperate Land Scheme of Dark Earth/Dark Green upper camouflage with Sky under-surfaces, note the curved demarcation from the radiator fairing to the lower section of the Perspex nose. The majority of B.IV Series I aircraft were delivered with their side cowlings painted entirely in Sky.

Upper left: Chief Test Pilot Geoffrey de Havilland Junior chats with workers. The first Mosquito bomber delivered to the RAF, W4064 served with 105 Squadron as 'GB-A'.

Upper right: The placing of the exhaust ejector nozzle and fairing (A) on the B.IV Series I differed to W4050; the rear section being angled slightly further downwards. The small vent (B) was added to improve cooling of the exhaust manifold rear ducting.

INSIDE THE B.IV SERIES I

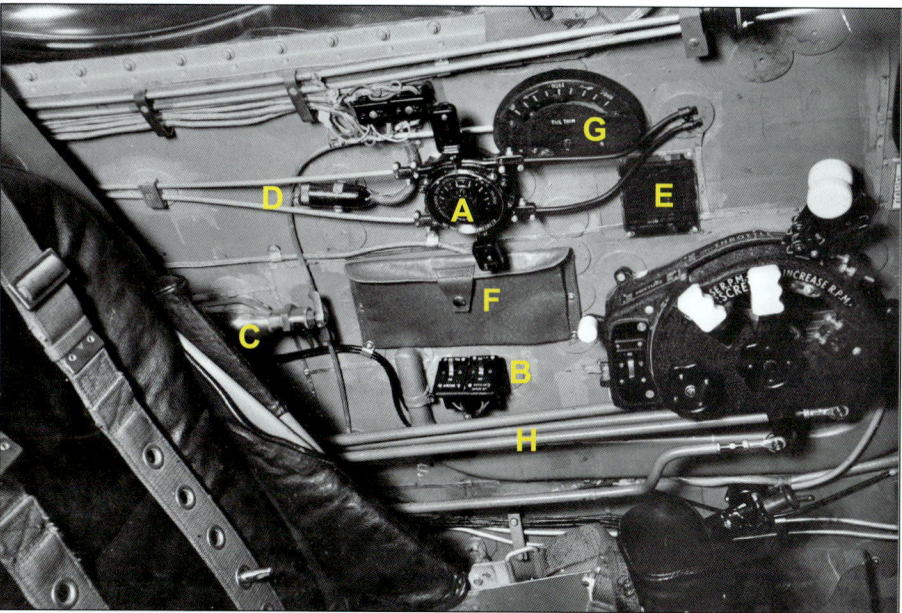

Left: Pilot's instrument panel and controls on a B.IV Series I showing the blind flying panel (1) in the centre with the engine instruments (2) grouped together on the left-hand side. Located on the cockpit wall is the engine control box with the throttle levers (3) mounted at the top, propeller pitch controls (4) on the side and the mixture control lever (5) at the rear; friction adjusting knobs for the throttle and pitch controls are positioned on the side of the box at (6) and (7). (8) is the control column yoke with the brake lever (9) visible immediately below the yoke's right arm. (10) is the group of four magneto switches, the two pairs of engine starter and booster coil push buttons positioned at (11) and (12) respectively. (13) is the rudder pedals; (14) is the bomb door selector lever: (15) is the undercarriage selector lever (the flap selector lever is immediately right of this but cannot be seen here) and (16) is the brake pressure gauge. Noteworthy are the support cushions (17) for the pilot's legs. The cockpit entrance hatch (18) is fully closed but the inner door is not visible, having been folded sideways to the right.

Above: Port side of the cockpit showing the TR9F radio controller (A), TR9F radio switches (B), fire extinguisher (C), intercommunication plug (D), engine data plate (E) plus a storage pouch for the 'pilot's miscellaneous articles' (F). Above the engine data plate is the elevator trim indicator (G). Note the throttle and pitch control linkage rods running aft from the engine control box (H).

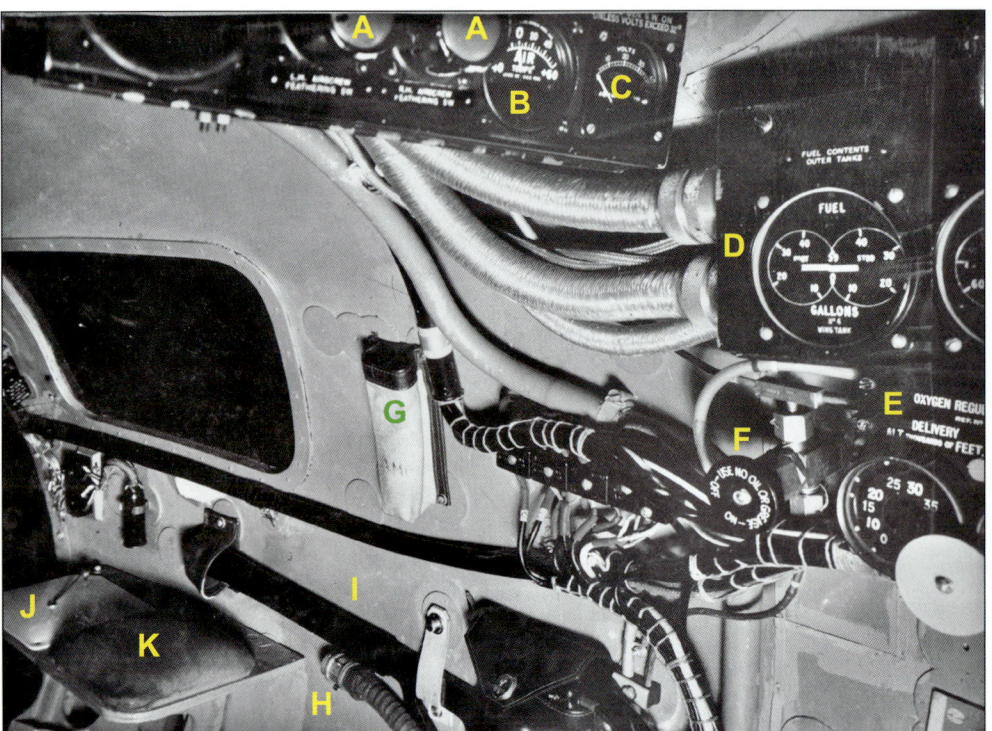

Left: The bomb aimer's position in the nose of a B.IV Series I showing the Mk. IXA3 Course Setting bomb sight (1) on its mounting bracket (2) built out from the port side of the fuselage. The bomb aimer's optically flat 'dry air sandwich' type windscreen (3) is directly below the bomb sight with its de-icing hand pump control above and behind (4). In the foreground is the automatic distributor box (5) with a Mk. II floodlamp (6) on the left-hand side and the bombing equipment fuse box on the right (7). Stowage for two emergency oxygen bottles was provided on the starboard side (8) while the oval shaped fitting on the Perspex nose housed the forward navigation lamp (9).

Above: View from the navigator's position of a B.IV Series I looking forward to the nose compartment. In the top left foreground is Junction Box A with the propeller feathering buttons (A), air temperature gauge (B) and voltmeter (C). At top right is the forward section of Junction Box B with the outer fuel tanks contents gauge (D), Mark VIII oxygen regulator (E) and the high-pressure oxygen valve (F). On the starboard cockpit wall is the stowage bag for the camera leads (G), navigator's oxygen bayonet socket (H) and the Fireman's crash axe (I). The navigator's writing tablet (J) and elbow rest (K) can be seen directly below the nose observation window.

Upper left: The starboard rear section of the bomb bay looking toward fuselage bulkhead four. Directly above the bomb crate (1) and bomb carrier (2) are the 68-gallon centre section fuel tanks (3). The fuel gallery (4) is mounted on the starboard fuselage side panel, the latter also carrying the hydraulic pipework (5).

Lower left: Another view of the bomb bay clearly showing the aft bomb crate (6) with its two Handley Page Type 5711 Q bomb carriers (7). Above the bomb door hydraulic rams (8) is the bomb loading winch (9) mounted in the rear compartment. The winch hoisting cable, with its ball end attachment (10), wound onto a deep grooved pulley driven by a sliding plate and pegs. When hoisting the bombs, the cable was threaded over separate pulleys at each crate, the ball end stowed in a clip (as seen here) when not in use. Note the observation lamp (11) on bulkhead four.

Upper right: The port side of the bomb bay, looking forward to fuselage bulkhead two, showing the front bomb crate (12) and bomb carriers (13). Various alternative bomb loads, consisting of 500lb and 250lb bombs and Mk. IA Small Bomb Containers, could be carried by the B.IV Series I up to a maximum of 1000lb. Only two 500lb bombs were carried, this being increased to four on Series II aircraft. Stencilled instructions on the bomb door denote the hoisting sequence for 250lb bombs (14), the hoisting cable position for 500 lb bombs (15) plus notification that Small Bomb Containers (or 250lb bombs) were only to be mounted on the forward bomb crate (16).

With its single-piece flaps lowered into the undercarriage nacelles, W4067 sits in the Hatfield flight shed awaiting delivery. Noteworthy is the aerial wire for the T.R.9F Transmitter Receiver, liberally covered in markers to prevent anybody inadvertently walking into it. On the Mosquito B.IV Series I this aerial wire ran from the port tailplane (A) to a connection on the inner trailing edge of the port wing (B), however on Series II aircraft it connected at the fixed aerial mast.

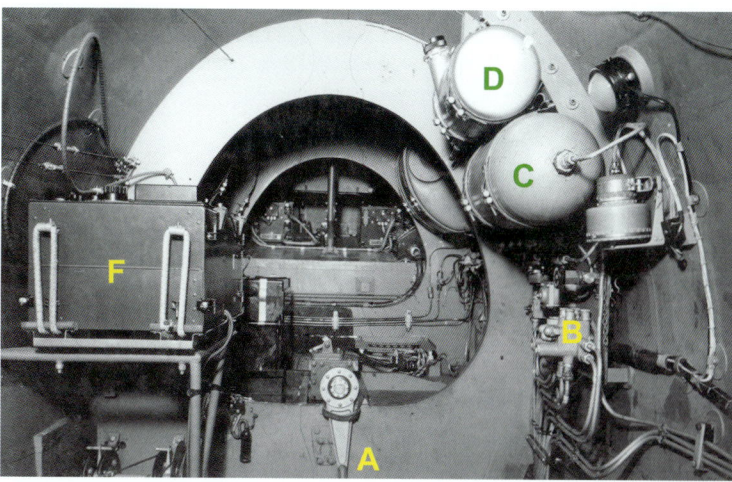

Main photo: Note the final production B.IV Series I W4072 features an extension of the upper surface camouflage down the engine side cowlings. Delivered to 105 Squadron W4072 was allocated the unit code letters 'GB-D', conducting the first bombing operation by a Mosquito when it attacked Cologne immediately following the initial "Thousand Bomber Raid".

Upper left: Like all B. IV's, W4072's featured single-disc brakes with slotted mainwheel hubs on port outer and starboard inner respectively (arrowed).

Upper right: Interior of a B.IV Series I looking forward to bulkhead four. Note the bomb winch handle (A), pneumatic and hydraulic panel (B), air bottle (C), de-icing fluid tank (D), hydraulic reservoir (E) and the T.R. 9F Transmitter Receiver (F).

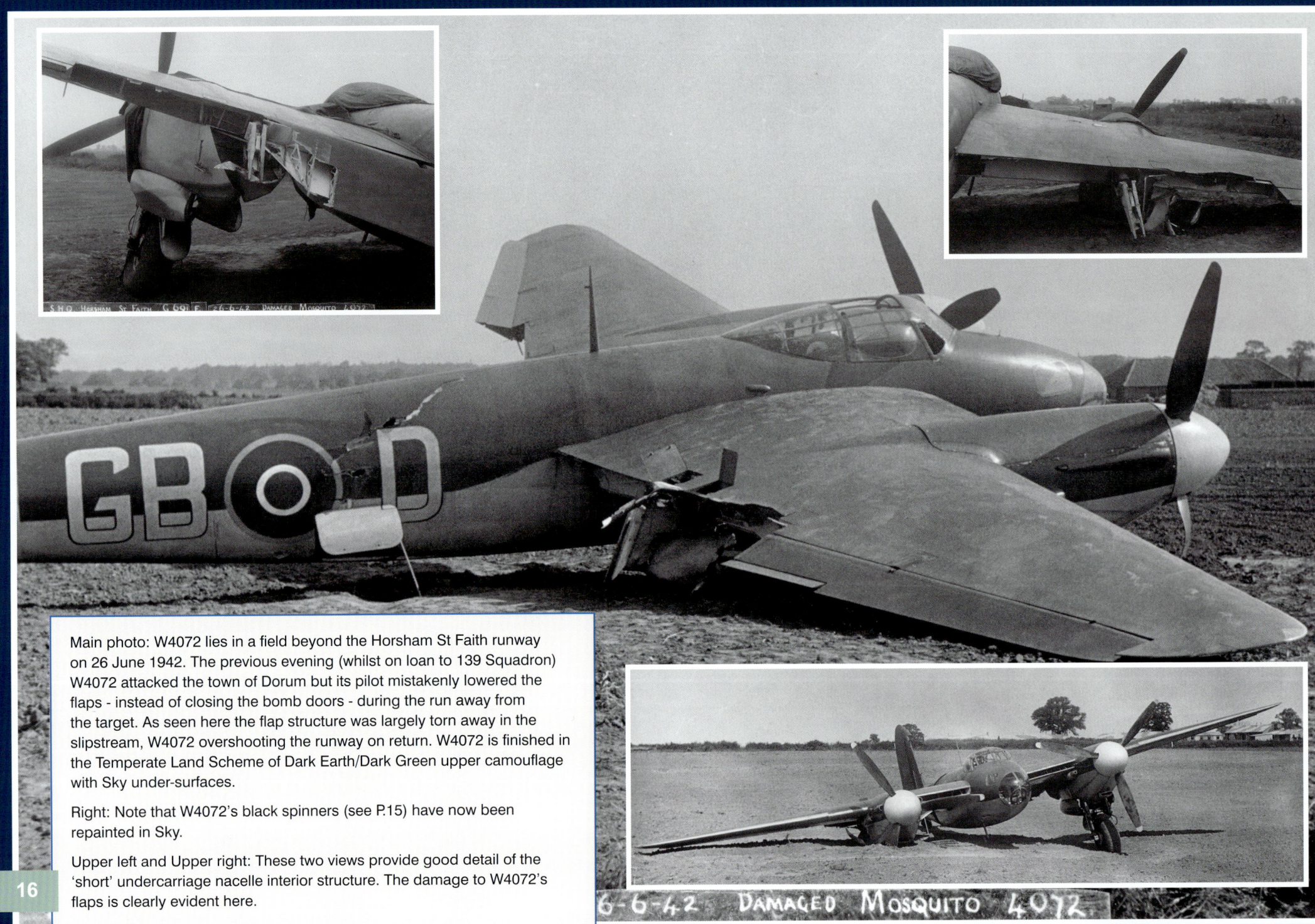

Main photo: W4072 lies in a field beyond the Horsham St Faith runway on 26 June 1942. The previous evening (whilst on loan to 139 Squadron) W4072 attacked the town of Dorum but its pilot mistakenly lowered the flaps - instead of closing the bomb doors - during the run away from the target. As seen here the flap structure was largely torn away in the slipstream, W4072 overshooting the runway on return. W4072 is finished in the Temperate Land Scheme of Dark Earth/Dark Green upper camouflage with Sky under-surfaces.

Right: Note that W4072's black spinners (see P.15) have now been repainted in Sky.

Upper left and Upper right: These two views provide good detail of the 'short' undercarriage nacelle interior structure. The damage to W4072's flaps is clearly evident here.

MOSQUITO B.IV SERIES I W4072, GB-D, 105 SQUADRON, JUNE 1942

MODELLER'S NOTES

Aircraft:
Final production B.IV Series I.
Short undercarriage nacelles with retracting rear section for operation of flaps.
'No.1 Tailplane' 19.5ft, 5.5in in span.
Fabric covered elevators.
Ducted exhaust system.
No longitudinal stiffening strake on starboard side of fuselage above rear access hatch.
'Round' tail wheel tyre.
Tear Drop' observation blisters on canopy side panels.
Navigation and Formation keeping lights on wingtips.
No ice guards on lower cowling carburettor air intakes.
Fixed aerial mast with Bakelite mounting ring surround.
Aerial wire for TR.9F transmitter receiver running from port tailplane to trailing edge of port wing.
No fairing fitted to windscreen de-icing jet nozzle on nose upper surface.
Trailing aerial tube beneath nose.
Two lamps mounted one above the other on extremity of tail cone (Formation Keeping and Navigation lamps respectively).
Single-disc brakes (with slotted mainwheel hubs on port outer, and starboard inner, respectively).

Discussion points:
Upper surface camouflage extends down engine side cowlings wrapping around exhaust exit ducts.
W4072 previously wore 42in diameter Type A fuselage roundels with equally spaced rings, plus 27in high by 24in wide fin flashes with equally spaced stripes.

17

The old and the new: 105 Squadron B.IV Series II's lined-up during a press day at Marham on 10 December 1942. The identity of the B.IV Series I landing in the background is something of a mystery. By this date only three B.IV Series I aircraft survived, W4057 with de Havilland at Hatfield, W4071 at Marham but undergoing repairs and W4072 which was then on the charge of 1655 Mosquito Training Unit. It seems likely that the aircraft seen here is W4072, suitably 'dressed up' for the occasion.

DAY BOMBERS B.IV SERIES II

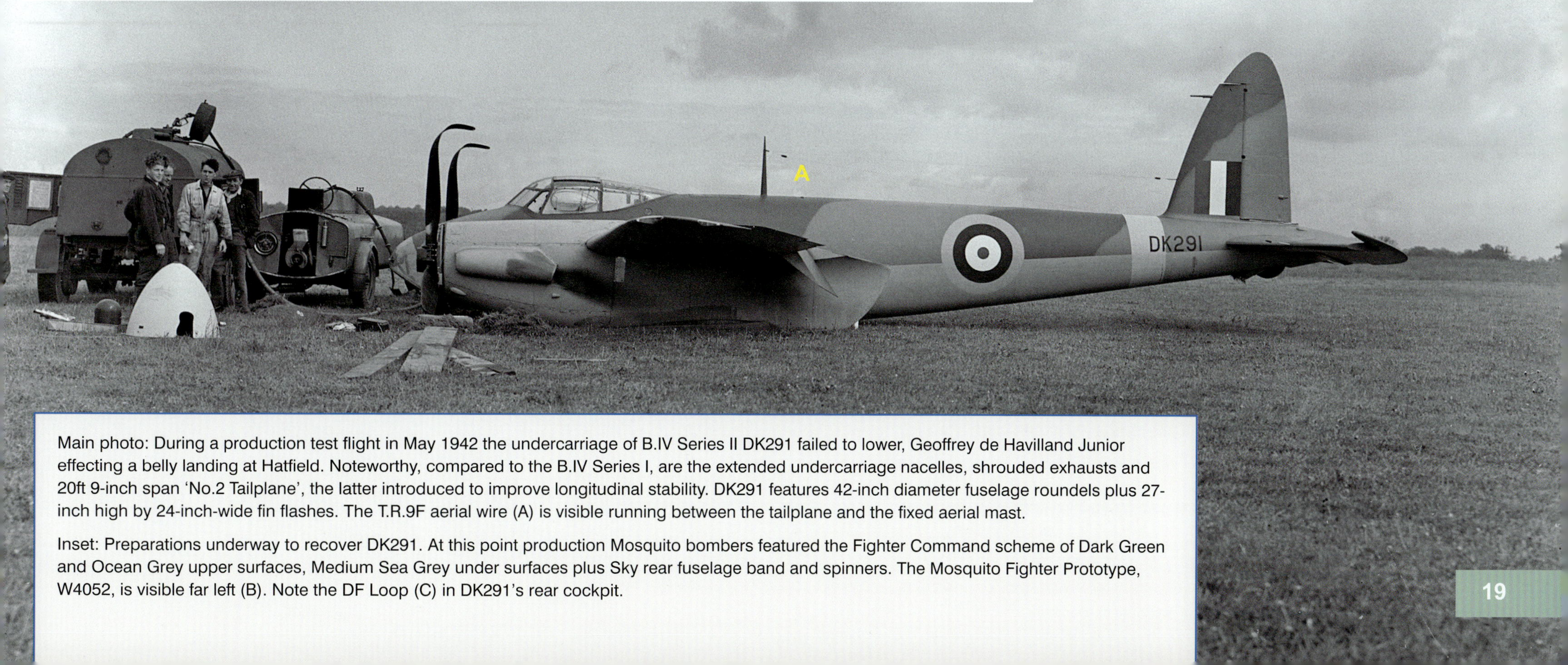

Main photo: During a production test flight in May 1942 the undercarriage of B.IV Series II DK291 failed to lower, Geoffrey de Havilland Junior effecting a belly landing at Hatfield. Noteworthy, compared to the B.IV Series I, are the extended undercarriage nacelles, shrouded exhausts and 20ft 9-inch span 'No.2 Tailplane', the latter introduced to improve longitudinal stability. DK291 features 42-inch diameter fuselage roundels plus 27-inch high by 24-inch-wide fin flashes. The T.R.9F aerial wire (A) is visible running between the tailplane and the fixed aerial mast.

Inset: Preparations underway to recover DK291. At this point production Mosquito bombers featured the Fighter Command scheme of Dark Green and Ocean Grey upper surfaces, Medium Sea Grey under surfaces plus Sky rear fuselage band and spinners. The Mosquito Fighter Prototype, W4052, is visible far left (B). Note the DF Loop (C) in DK291's rear cockpit.

FLAPS AND NACELLES

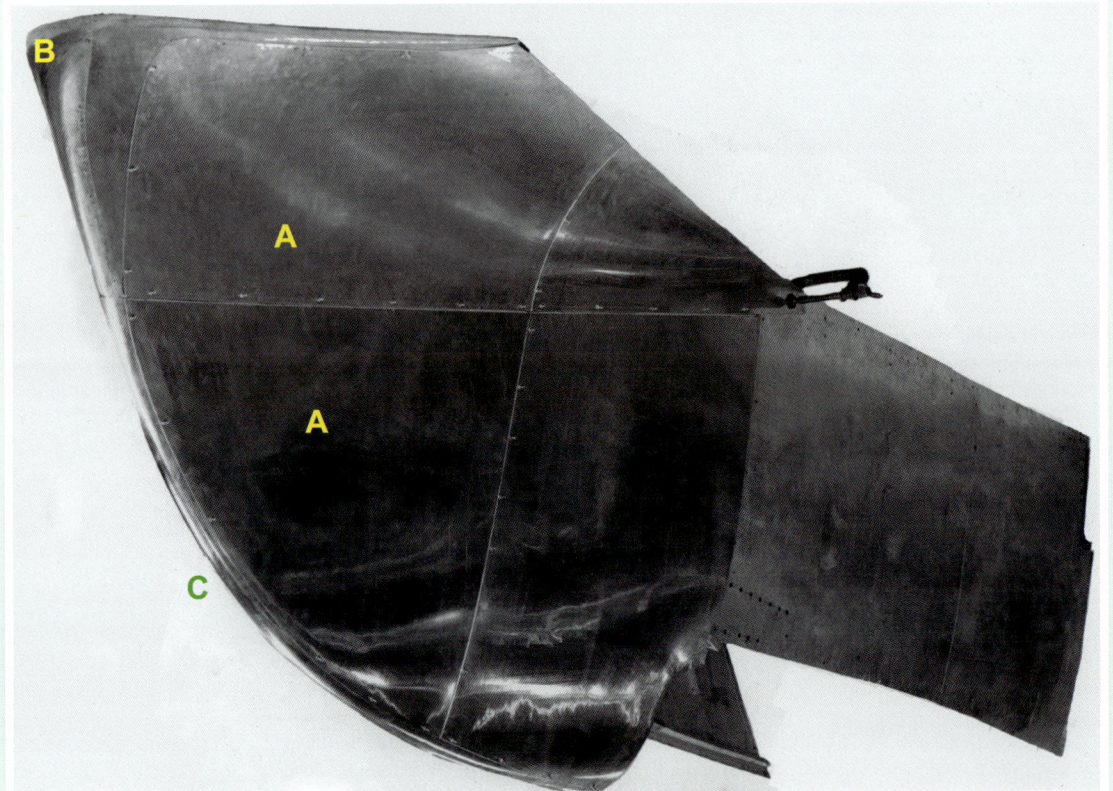

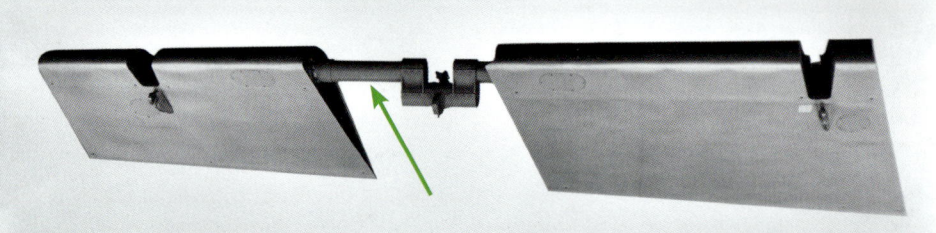

Four photos illustrating the modifications necessary to introduce extended undercarriage nacelles on production Mosquitoes:

Above: The extension to the nacelle rear section (A), gently curving to a point at the tip (B). The extensions comprised of riveted aluminium panels attached to an aluminium keel (C).

Upper right: B.IV Series II DK291 (see page 19) clearly illustrates protrusion of the extended nacelle beyond the trailing edge of the wing. The unpainted panel (arrowed) is the flap hydraulic jack inspection door.

Centre right: To allow for the nacelle extension the flaps were split into inboard and outboard sections linked by a torque tube (arrowed). The torque tube featured a cranked fitting incorporating both the centre hinge plus a connecting lug for the hydraulic operating jack.

Lower right: Looking down on the starboard flap with the hydraulic jack inspection door removed. The inboard (1) and outboard (2) flaps are either side of the nacelle extension (3). with their connecting torque tube (4) in the centre. Note the operating hydraulic jack (5) plus the aileron control cable (6), the latter running through the flap shroud box on the rear spar.

DK290/G, the seventh production B.IV Series II (see page 39), wears Fighter Command special recognition markings consisting of Sky spinners, Sky rear fuselage band and yellow wing leading edge stripes. This was a short-lived attempt to confuse German fighters as to the unarmed status of Mosquito bombers, additionally helping distinguish the Mosquito from the Messerschmitt Me 210. Unusual for a B.IV Series II, in connection with trials to measure exhaust propulsion effect, DK290/G is equipped with six exhaust stacks on the engine outboard side.

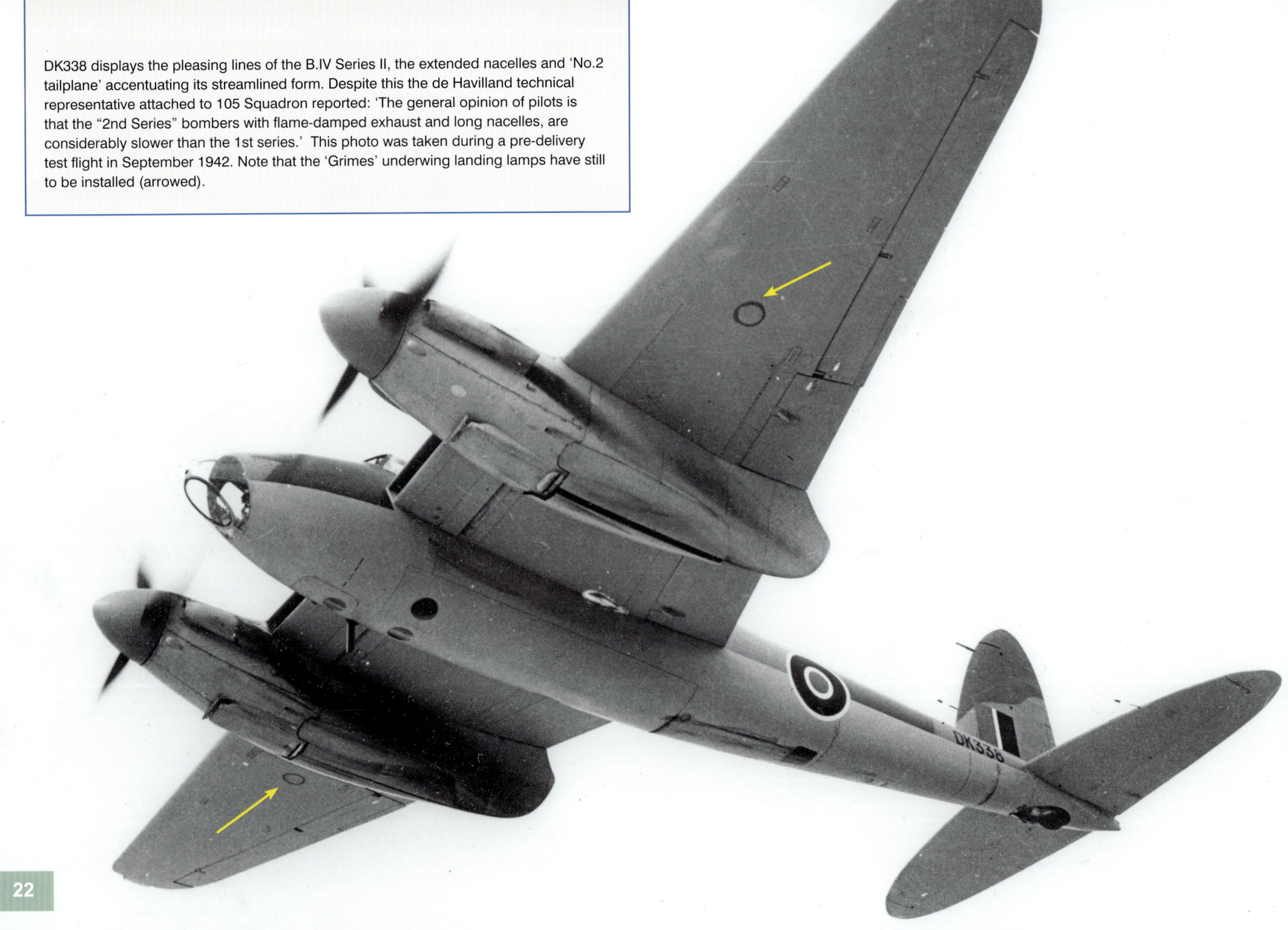

DK338 displays the pleasing lines of the B.IV Series II, the extended nacelles and 'No.2 tailplane' accentuating its streamlined form. Despite this the de Havilland technical representative attached to 105 Squadron reported: 'The general opinion of pilots is that the "2nd Series" bombers with flame-damped exhaust and long nacelles, are considerably slower than the 1st series.' This photo was taken during a pre-delivery test flight in September 1942. Note that the 'Grimes' underwing landing lamps have still to be installed (arrowed).

Below: The B.IV Series I and II could be equipped with two cameras in the bomb bay forward section, perspex windows being fitted in the bomb doors to provide for this. Alcad discs covered the windows when cameras were not installed. Note the drain holes forward of fuselage bulkhead 2 (arrowed).

Right: A well-known but nevertheless stunning view of 105 Squadron B.IV Series II DZ367 'GB-J' peeling away from the camera. Noteworthy are the plate type air thermometer beneath the nose (A), the rear fuselage F.24 camera window (B) plus the red, green, and amber downward identification lights at (C), (D) and (E) respectively.

Main photo: 105 Squadron B.IV Series II's (top to bottom) DZ367 'GB-J', DZ353 'GB-E' and DZ360 'GB-A' running up at Marham during the Press Day on 10 December 1942. Note the absence of Sky spinners and rear fuselage band (see P.19), the scheme for Mosquito bombers having been standardised as Dark Green and Ocean Grey upper surfaces with Medium Sea Grey under surfaces. The fuselage roundels are 36-inch diameter national marking III and the fin flash 24 inches square with narrow white band. Squadron codes are approximately 30 inches high and applied in Sky, with the serial number in black 8 inches high. The filler cap for the front long range fuel tank is visible (arrowed).

Main photo: With B.IV Series II DZ360 'GB-A' as a backdrop, 105 Squadron armourers tend to a train of 500lb bombs at Marham. On 22 December 1942 DZ360 took off for a raid on engine sheds at Termonde but was shot down by anti-aircraft fire near Axel in the Netherlands. The crew access ladder (which was telescopic and stored in a compartment within the forward fuselage) is just visible beyond the starboard undercarriage nacelle.

Inset: Airman cleaning the Perspex nose of a well-worn 105 Squadron B.IV Series II at Marham. The Perspex nose was manufactured in two halves joined along the centre line (top and bottom) by capping strips (A) with the bomb aimer's optically flat glass panel fitted in the centre (B). On later bomber and photographic reconnaissance variants the Perspex nose was 'blown' as a single unit, being slightly longer and more bulbous in its forward section. Note the glycol de-icing spray tube above the bomb aimer's glass panel (C).

Armourer checking the tail fusing of a 500lb bomb on a B.IV Series II. As illustrated here, four short tailed 500lb bombs could be accommodated by the B.IV Series II, the port side rear bomb being hoisted first followed by the port side forward bomb. The starboard rear and front bombs then followed respectively, hoisting instructions being outlined on a placard attached to the port bomb bay door (A). Note that the bomb door top skins are dished (B) to allow ½ inch clearance for the rear pair of 500lb bombs. The tube for the trailing aerial is visible at top left (C).

DZ353 'GB-E' of 105 Squadron, probably the most celebrated of all B.IV Series II's, appearing as the subject of countless wartime drawings, models, and photographs. Initially delivered to 105 Squadron, DZ353 passed to 139 Squadron in September 1943 before allocation to 627 Squadron two months later. During an attack on Rennes on 8 June 1944, DZ353 was hit by flak over the target and crashed between Orgeres and St. Erblon.

Visible beneath the rear cockpit is the external fairing (arrowed) for the starboard 'Joint A' fuselage to wing attachment point.

With oil streaks covering the nacelles, undercarriage doors and tailplane, DZ353 banks away during a photographic sortie in December 1942. Note the demarcation line (arrowed) between the fore and aft sections of under wing madapolam covering. The eagle eyed will notice the absence of a longitudinal stiffening strake above the rear fuselage access hatch (see P.33). Note the original round (sometimes referred to as a 'balloon') tailwheel tyre, a feature of all early production Mosquitoes)

Right: Detailed close-up depicting the starboard side of a B.IV Series II on the Hatfield production line in early 1942. Noteworthy are the cowling panel ring (A); 'tear drop' shaped canopy observation blister (B); Direction Finding (DF) Loop (C); Ki-Gass priming pump access door (D); engine hand-crank point (E) plus the starboard engine right magneto (F).

Below: Port side of the same B.IV Series II showing the coolant header tank (1); coolant pipe from the header tank to the circulating pump (2); coolant header tank relief valve (3); capillary coils (4); duct for fuel pump cooling air (5); boost gauge fuel trap (6); engine accessories drain tank (7); jacking point (8) and magneto cooling air pipe (9).

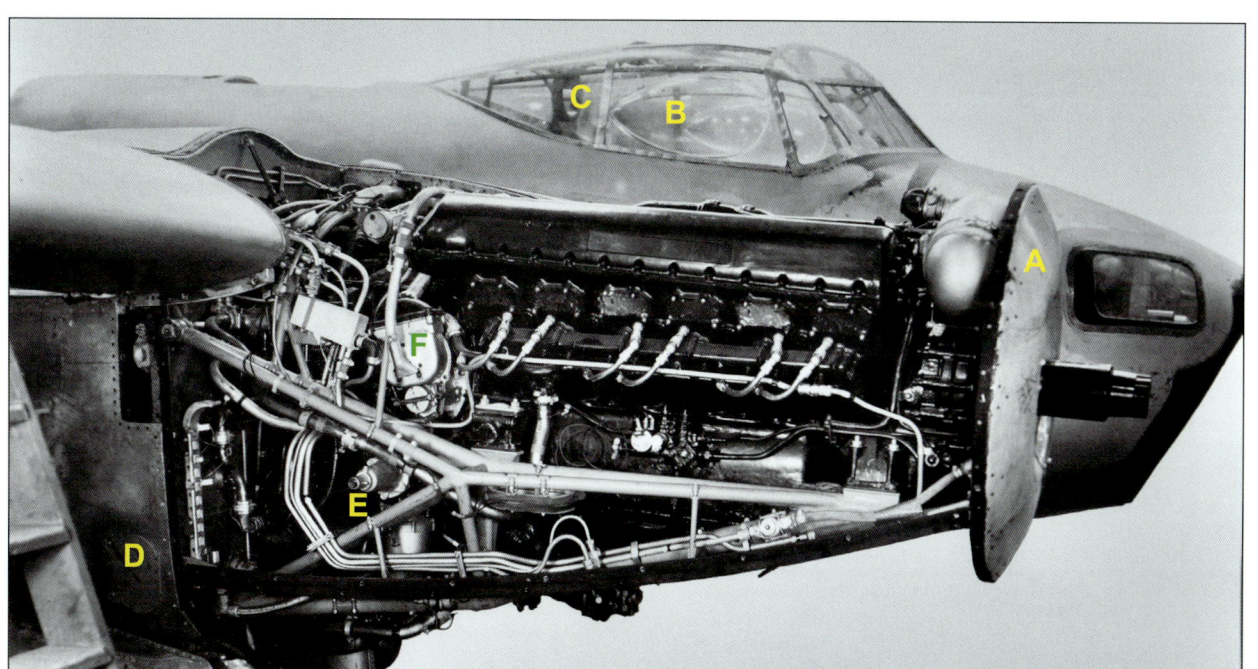

Another B.IV Series II production line image, this one from an earlier stage in the assembly process. Note the bomb aimer's emergency oxygen bottle stowage (1) plus the bomb-aimer's writing tablet (2) and elbow support (3). Behind these is the camera leads storage bag (4), rear loop for the Fireman's crash axe handle (5) and the Very cartridge stowage rack (6). Built out from the port side of the fuselage is the rudder pedals box (7) plus the mounting rack for the bomb sight (8). Visible on the starboard side of the cockpit wall are several circular shaped discs known as 'ferrules' (9). Designed for attaching interior fittings to the fuselage, ferrules comprised a plywood disc mounted on an ebonite or wood plug. Within the plug a threaded brass insert was set with its open end in the disc centre, the ferrules affixed by tacks through the plywood disc. (10) is the oil cooler, (11) is the radiator and (12) is the cabin heater. The windscreen panels and canopy side glazing have still to be installed.

Final assembly of late production B.IV Series II Mosquitoes at Hatfield in May 1943.

Upper right: With the nose slung at bulkhead two (the rear sling will be at bulkhead five) a B.IV Series II fuselage is readied for mating to its wing. Note the jury strut (arrowed) bridging the 'wing gap' between bulkheads two and three. Necessary to temporarily brace the structure, the jury strut was removed in the final stages of lowering the fuselage onto the wing. A 'floating' side panel occupied the lower void between bulkheads two and three once the wing was in position.

Lower right: Female factory workers prepare a Merlin 21 for installation in a B.IV Series II. The coolant header tank (1) is resting on top of the engine

Below: Now on its undercarriage, a B.IV Series II in the last stages of assembly. At this point a test was made of the coolant system followed by a complete final inspection. The aircraft was then despatched to the paint shop where the tailplane, fin and rudder, flaps, ailerons and rear access hatch would receive their final finish. Note the early batch of Mosquito FB.VI's taking shape in the background.

 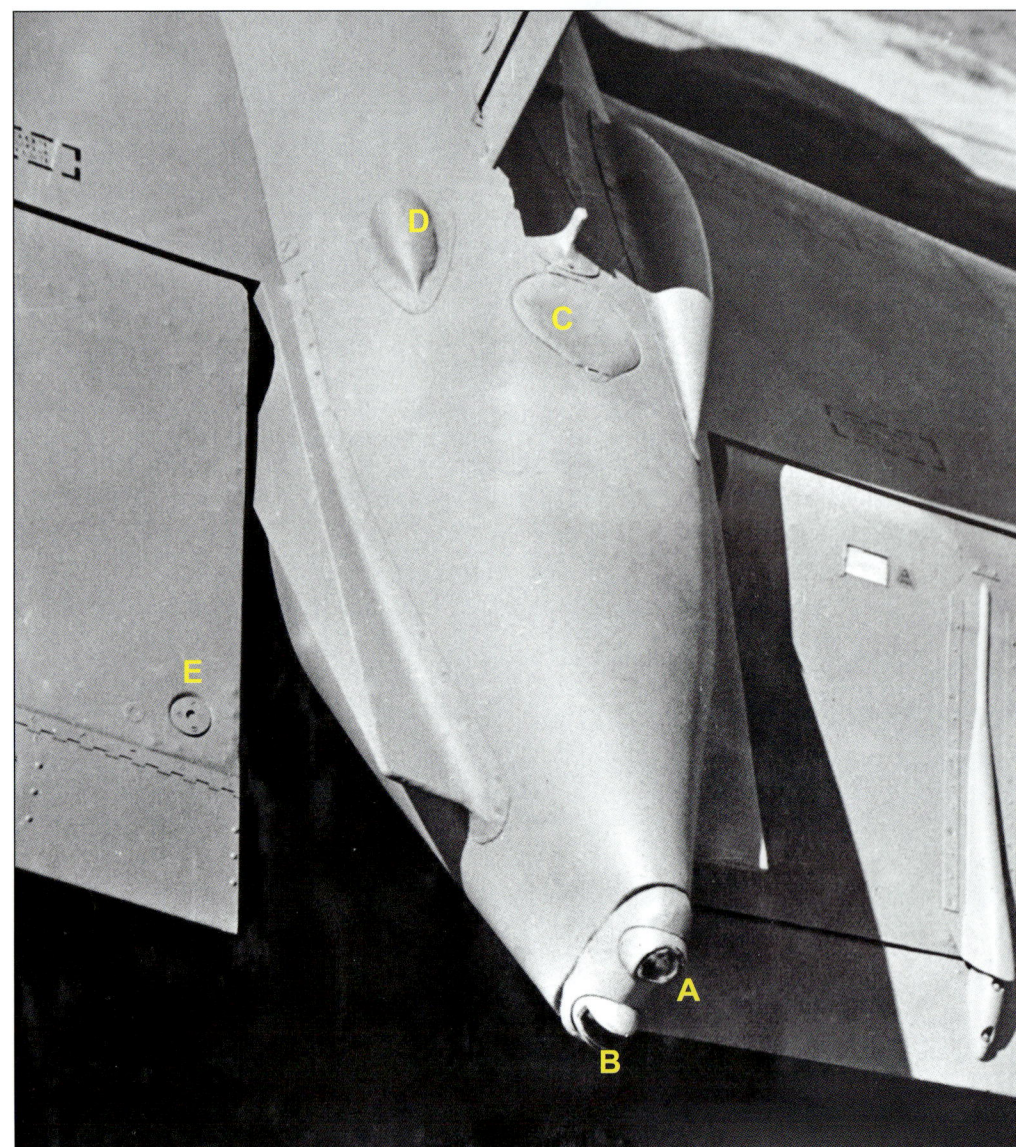

Upper left: The rear fuselage of a B.IV Series II on the Hatfield assembly line in late May 1943. This is looking directly onto the rear of bulkhead seven mounted to which are the tailplane (1) and tailwheel (2). The lower pair of tailplane adjustable support tubes are at (3) with the tailwheel mudguard at (4). (5) are the rudder trim cables and (6) the elevator cables, the port elevator trim tab being visible at (7). Note the earlier round (or 'balloon') tailwheel tyre has now been replaced by the double ridged Marstrand anti-shimmy unit (8).

Upper right: The tailcone of B.IV Series II DZ313 showing the navigation lamp (A) and formation keeping lamp (B) on its extremity. The formation keeping lamp would later be deleted following the introduction of RESIN (Restricted Intensity) lights on the wingtips. (C) is the inspection panel for the elevator centre hinge and (D) is the fairing for the elevator cables torque shaft lever. The recess for the port elevator gust lock can be seen at (E).

Above: The second Mosquito bomber squadron was No.139, two of their B.IV Series II's, DZ421 'XD-Bar G' and DZ464 'XD-C', seen here. 139 initially borrowed aircraft from 105 Squadron but operated its own Mosquitoes from December 1942.

Inset right: B.IV Series II's of 139 Squadron running up at Marham, nearest the camera is DZ421 'XD-G' (but minus the Bar above the G as seen above). Note that DZ421 features a longitudinal stiffening strake above the rear fuselage access hatch (arrowed). As 'Mod 167', the stiffening strake was introduced on production Mosquitoes from December 1942 and reinforced the fuselage monocoque shell above the weak point of the hatch cut out, existing aircraft being retrofitted. This weakness was first identified following an incident with W4050 during A&AEE trials in February 1941.

Main photo: Another photo of 139 Squadron B.IV Series II DZ464 'XD-C', by now equipped with exhaust stubs in place of its original flame damping shrouds (see P.43). Delivered to 139 Squadron on 29 January 1943, DZ464 had a relatively short career, being shot down by flak over the French coast while returning from a raid on Orleans on 12 May 1943. Note that the fixed aerial mast has been removed. The stiffening strake above the rear access hatch is clearly visible.

Inset right: During a daylight raid on Ijmuiden on 22 September 1942, 105 Squadron B.IV Series II DK337 'GB-N' incurred light flak damage to the starboard fuselage and inner flap, half of the flap top skin being blown away. Note the open rear access hatch (arrowed).

139 Squadron B.IV Series II DZ470 'XD-N' in early 1943. Note the fabric covered elevators (with the starboard unit's inspection panel at (1)). In January 1944 'Mod 284' was introduced replacing fabric covered elevators with metal skinned units on all variants of Mosquito (with the exception of the PR. I and B.IV Series I). The bulge on the tailcone (2) is the fairing for the elevator static balance weight.

Main photo: With its pitot mast covered (arrowed), DZ470 undergoes a compass swing at Marham. Delivered to 139 Squadron on 5th February 1943, DZ470 was regularly crewed by Flg Off C.V. Pereira and Flg Off G.H. Gilbert. This aircraft was lost on its fifteenth sortie, an attack on engine sheds at Mechelen on 11 April 1943. Note the ice guard on the starboard lower cowling carburettor air intake (1) plus the handle for the signal pistol (2) just visible in the canopy roof.

Inset above: Flg Off C.V. Pereira (right) and Flg Off G.H. Gilbert (left) by the nose of DZ470 at Marham. Judging by the small tally of bomb symbols on the nose, this photo would appear to date from early spring 1943. The small plate (3) on the starboard inner engine cowling reads: 'Engine must not be run without exhaust shrouds'. Note the plate type air thermometer under the nose (4).

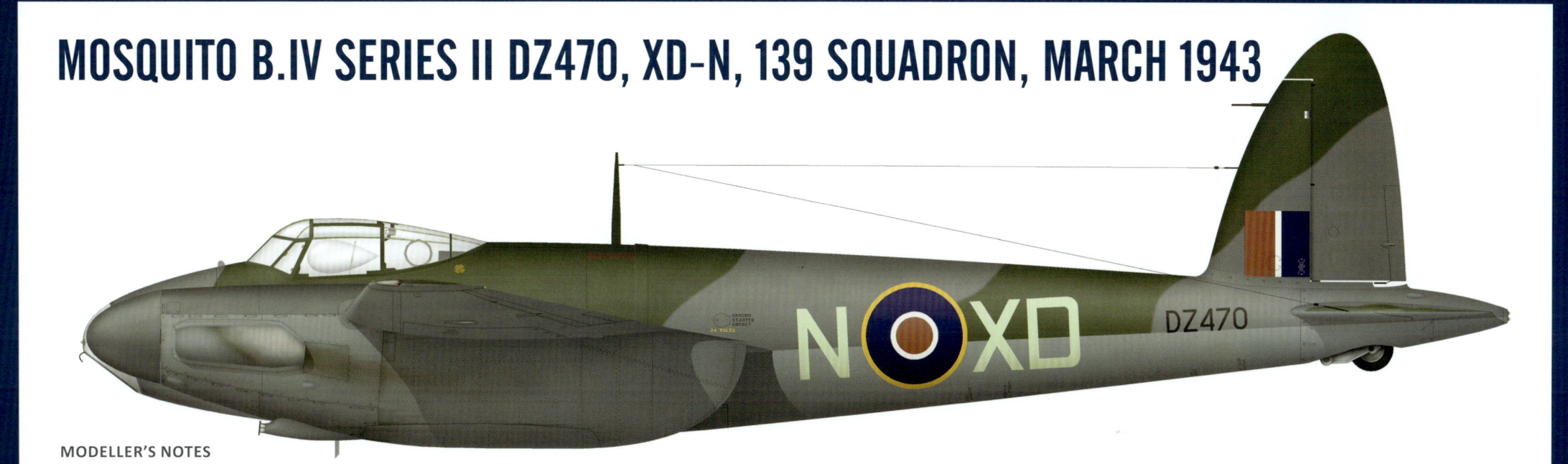

MOSQUITO B.IV SERIES II DZ470, XD-N, 139 SQUADRON, MARCH 1943

MODELLER'S NOTES

Aircraft:
Mid production B.IV Series II.
Long undercarriage nacelles extending beyond wing trailing edge.
'No.2 Tailplane' 20ft 9in in span.
Fabric covered elevators.
'Saxophone' exhausts contained within flame damping shrouds.
Longitudinal stiffening strake on starboard side of fuselage above rear access hatch.
'Round' tail wheel tyre.
'Tear Drop' observation blisters on canopy side panels.
Navigation and Formation keeping lights on wingtips.
Fixed aerial mast with Bakelite mounting ring surround.
Ice guards on lower cowling carburettor air intakes.
Aerial wire for TR.9F transmitter receiver running from port tailplane to fixed aerial mast.
Fairing fitted to windscreen de-icing jet nozzle on nose upper surface.
Trailing aerial tube beneath nose.
Two lamps mounted one above the other on extremity of tail cone (Formation Keeping and Navigation lamps respectively).
Inconel heat resistant panel inserts on engine side cowlings, aft of exhaust shrouds.
Single-disc brakes (with slotted mainwheel hubs on port outer, and starboard inner, respectively).
Six bomb symbols on the nose, possibly in yellow.
Straight demarcation line for nose camouflage.

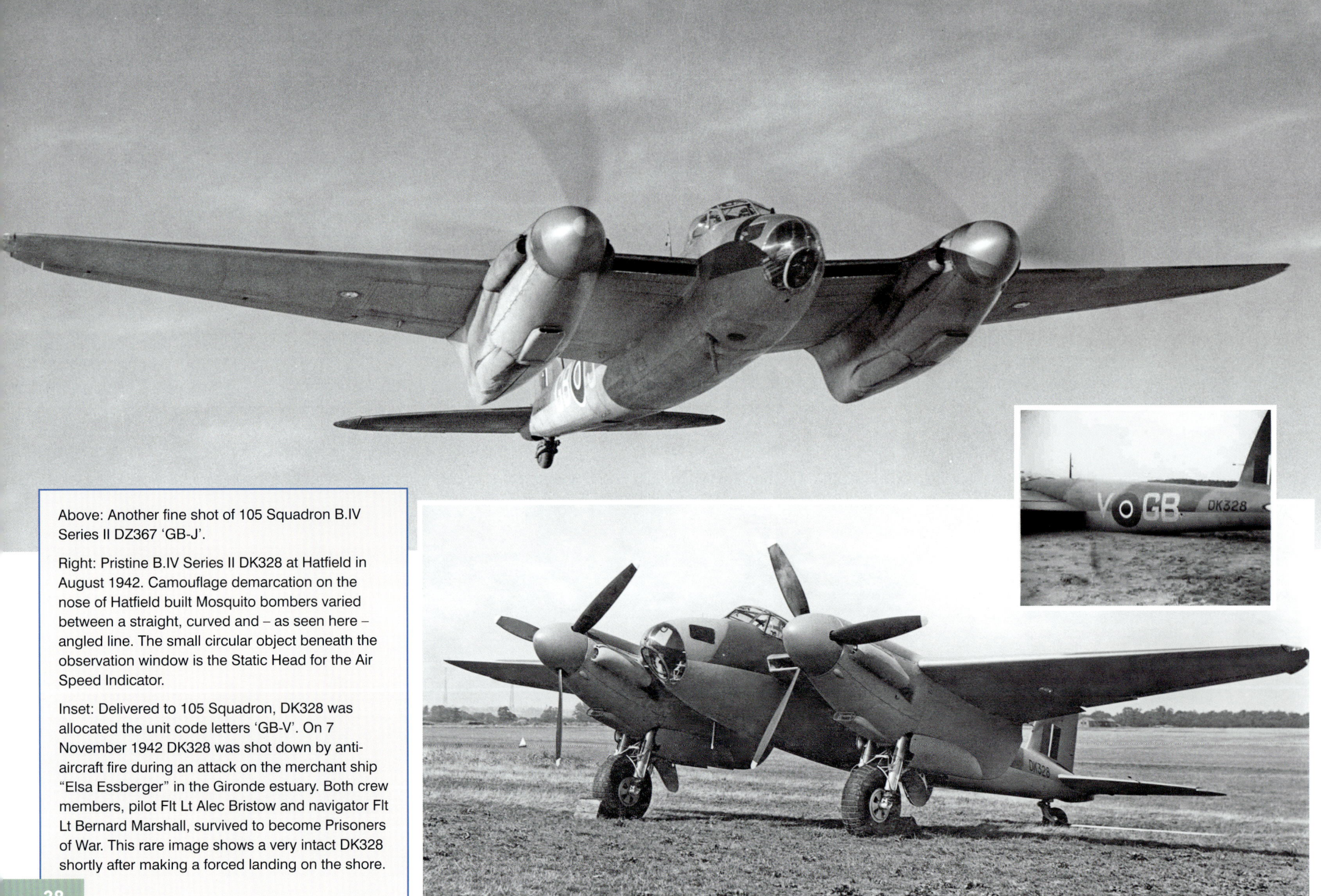

Above: Another fine shot of 105 Squadron B.IV Series II DZ367 'GB-J'.

Right: Pristine B.IV Series II DK328 at Hatfield in August 1942. Camouflage demarcation on the nose of Hatfield built Mosquito bombers varied between a straight, curved and – as seen here – angled line. The small circular object beneath the observation window is the Static Head for the Air Speed Indicator.

Inset: Delivered to 105 Squadron, DK328 was allocated the unit code letters 'GB-V'. On 7 November 1942 DK328 was shot down by anti-aircraft fire during an attack on the merchant ship "Elsa Essberger" in the Gironde estuary. Both crew members, pilot Flt Lt Alec Bristow and navigator Flt Lt Bernard Marshall, survived to become Prisoners of War. This rare image shows a very intact DK328 shortly after making a forced landing on the shore.

HIGHBALL

Below: DK290 served as a development airframe employed for tests of longitudinal stability at higher weights, speed trials with flame damping exhaust stubs, plus trial installation of the 'Highball' bouncing bomb. In connection with the stability tests, DK290 is equipped with enlarged elevator horn balances (arrowed) equal to 9.8% of the elevator area aft of the hinge line (normal elevators were 6.9%).

Inset left: In March 1943 DK290 was assigned to Heston Aircraft for trial installation of the 'Highball' bouncing bomb, two mock-up 'Highballs' being installed (in tandem) within the highly modified bomb bay.

39

Above: Another view of DK290 equipped with enlarged elevator horn balances and prior to the installation of 'Highball'. During longitudinal stability trials DK290 tested a dihedral tailplane, this later being replaced by the experimental 'No.3 tailplane' spanning 21ft 3.5inches. Note the overpainted outer ring of DK290's original 42-inch diameter fuselage roundel.

Below: A fine study of DK290 equipped with the 'mock-up' 'Highball' installation in 1943. Some thirty-one B.IV Series II's were subsequently modified (by Vickers, Airspeed and Marshalls) for 618 Squadron's intended carrier borne anti-shipping role in the Pacific Theatre, the squadron sailing to Australia in October 1944. Note the 'G' suffix now applied to DK290's serial number, this signified the aircraft should be guarded when not flown.

618 Squadron 'Highball' B. IV's practicing carrier deck landings and take-offs aboard HMS Implacable in 1944. Each Mosquito was equipped with Merlin 25's and four bladed propellers, heavier gauge undercarriage leg casings, and twin brake unit main wheels. Armoured windscreens were also fitted along with provision for two 'Highballs' in the converted bomb bay. To withstand the heavier loads imposed by deck landings, structural alterations were made to the fuselage, these also facilitating installation of the 'Vee' frame arrestor hook.

Right: This is believed to be DZ537 'VY' taking off from HMS 'Implacable' on 6 September 1944. DZ537 is finished in the standard bomber scheme of Dark Green and Ocean Grey upper surfaces with Medium Sea Grey under surfaces, the latter later being altered to Azure Blue.

Upper left: With its arrestor hook lowered, an unidentified Mosquito lands aboard 'Implacable'. The fuselage armour plating (arrowed) on 'Highball' B. IV's cut off access to the nose compartment, aiming of the weapon being undertaken with a bespoke sight mounted in the cockpit.

Upper right: Another B.IV prepares to take off from 'Implacable' on 10 October 1944, evidence suggests this is DZ542. Note the four bladed propellers.

41

EXHAUSTS

Right: W4072's port outer side cowling illustrates the main features of the B.IV Series I's ducted exhaust system with its angled ejector nozzle and fairing (1), manifold cooling intake (2) plus the small vent (3) to improve cooling of the manifold rear ducting.

Lower left: The ducted exhaust system with the side cowling removed, note the cooling vent intake for the rear section (4) plus the ejector nozzle (5). Problems with the ducted exhaust system led to its replacement by either 'saxophone' manifolds, enclosed within flame damping shrouds, or individual exhaust stubs.

Below: Dated 15 January 1942 this illustrates an early version of the 'saxophone' exhaust manifold, probably on bomber prototype W4057. Developed for use on single-stage Merlin Mosquito bombers and night fighters, the 'saxophone' featured two 'fishtail' stubs (6) enclosed within a flame damping shroud on the side cowling (see P.43). In this photo the shroud has been removed from the cowling but its outline remains visible.

Inset: The production form of 'saxophone' manifold shown with the side cowling removed. Note the exhaust inner shroud (arrowed).

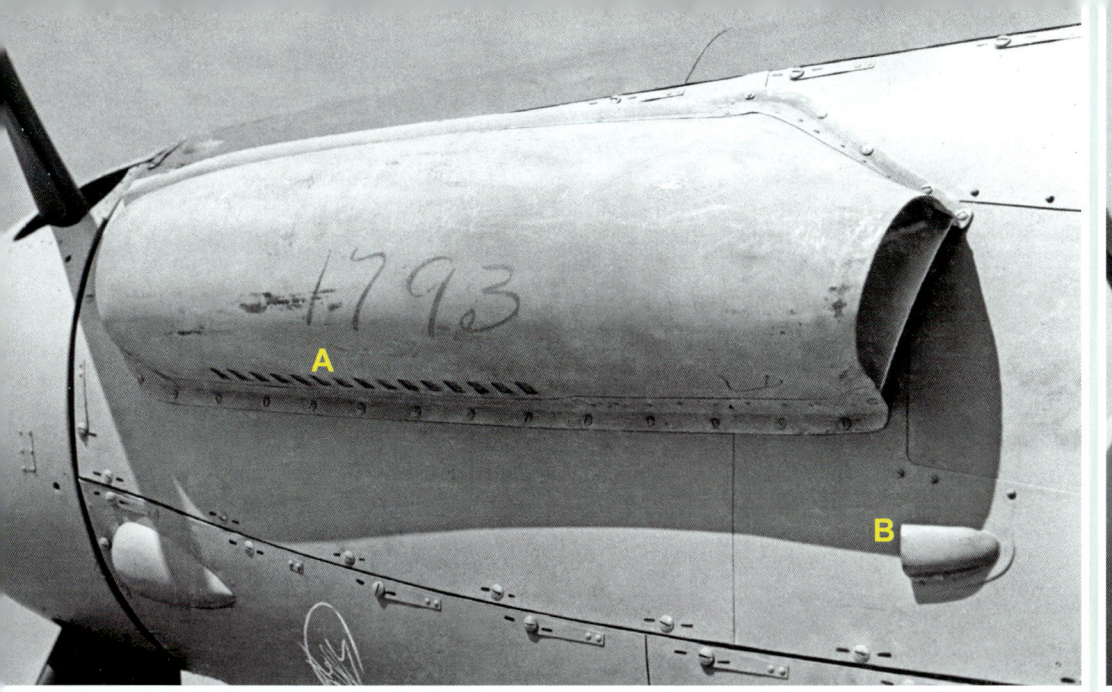

Upper left: The 'saxophone' exhaust system's flame damping shroud attached to the engine side cowling. A line of small ducts on the lower section (A) provided cooling air for the two 'fishtail' stubs. (B) is the fuel pump cooling duct.

Left: It was unusual to see six exhaust stubs on the engine outboard side of British built single stage Merlin Mosquitoes, the final production standard being five. On the engine inboard side, the radiator structure extended forward of the mainplane leading edge, physically prohibiting the installation of a separate stub on the rearmost cylinder. Therefore, the last two stubs were 'Siamesed' into one, angled to eject beneath the oil cooler section of the radiator structure. To standardise production of exhaust inners shrouds, plus exhaust stub 'slots on cowling side panel jigs, the same layout was repeated on the engine outboard side. However, before this was finalised, several B.IV Series II's, PR. IV's and F. II's featured six stubs on the outboard side. Additionally, the six outboard stub layout was standard on all Australian built single-stage Merlin Mosquitoes. This photo depicts DK290 during tests to evaluate flame-damping qualities of de Havilland designed 'fish tail' stubs. Note the magneto cooling duct (C) plus extension of the upper surface camouflage down the entire side cowling.

Upper right: A late production B.IV Series II showing the standard five stub exhaust layout on the engine outboard side. Note the inconel heat resistant panel (D) on the side cowling rear section. (E) is the cooling duct for the exhaust manifold flanges and (F) is the Spark Plug Cooling Duct.

This 105 Squadron B.IV Series II (believed to be DK336) also has six exhaust stubs on the engine outboard side, the strengthening plate on the side cowling (1) featuring an extended 'slot' for the rearmost stub. It was realised early on that stub exhausts created enough exhaust propulsion effect to boost maximum speed by 10 -13 mph. Stub exhausts produced more glare so 105 Squadron (as it operated between dawn and dusk) requested fifteen aircraft with shrouds and three with stubs. Note the blister covering the engine hand crank point (2), the magneto cooling intake (3) and the Inconel heat resistant panel (4).

OBOE

Above: The first Mosquito to be equipped with OBOE was B.IV Series II DK300 of 109 Squadron, seen here at Stradishall in July 1942. OBOE was a precision blind bombing system enabling accurate attacks through cloud cover. Employing secondary radar principles, it consisted of a 'cat' and 'mouse' ground station (each roughly 100 miles apart) emitting pulses on a single carrier frequency but with different recurrence frequencies. The 'cat' directed the Mosquito's track while the 'mouse' calculated and signalled the moment of bomb release. An early production B.IV Series II, DK300 originally wore the Sky rear fuselage band, seen overpainted in this photo. Note the lack of a fairing on the windscreen de-icing jet nozzle (arrowed).

Inset right: The nose of DK300 showing the OBOE equipment installation racks. The Perspex nose and side windows of OBOE equipped Mosquito bombers were later overpainted to conceal the top-secret secret equipment inside. Note the absence of a glycol de-icing spray tube above the bomb aimer's flat glass panel, this being no longer required.

Left: DZ319 'HS-H', an OBOE equipped B.IV of 109 Squadron, photographed at Little Staughton after completing its 101st sortie. On 20 December 1942 DZ319 took part in the first OBOE operation, an attack on the coking plant at Lutterade in Holland. The bomb aimer's Perspex nose and side windows have been painted over; the aircraft's individual code 'H' displayed in red on the flat glass panel. DZ319 features Dark Green and Ocean Grey upper surface camouflage with Night under surface finish, the latter extending up the fuselage sides, applied as per DTD Technical Circular Pattern No.2. The mission tally bomb symbols are believed to be in red with yellow outlines. Note the shrouded exhausts and 'needle' blade propellers.

Right: B.IV Series II DZ518 'AZ-F' forms the backdrop to this 627 Squadron air and ground crew line up at Oakington in January 1944. The sole marker squadron in 5 Group, 627 Squadron employed a visual means of target marking instead of the more technical equipment (such as OBOE and G-H) used by 8 Group. This technique took a great deal of practice, but accuracy became so dependable that – to quote one former 627 Squadron aircrew member - 'we grew from a toy airplane to a lethal weapon'. DZ518 also features Dark Green and Ocean Grey upper surface camouflage with Night under surface finish extending up the fuselage sides. Note the bomb sight in the nose plus the unshrouded exhausts. DZ518 served with 105 and 139 Squadrons before passing to 627 in December 1943.

B.IV SERIES II COCKPIT

Left: Taken on the Hatfield production line in March 1943, this photograph shows the pilot's instrument panel and controls on a B.IV Series II. Basically, identical to the B.IV Series I (see P.11), in the centre is the blind flying panel (1) with the engine instrumentation on the left-hand side (2). Beneath the blind flying panel are the engine starter (3) and booster coil push buttons (4), the group of four magneto switches (5), the undercarriage position indicator (6) and the flap position indicator (7). The oxygen regulator is at (8) and the brake pressure gauge at (9). To the right of the oxygen regulator is the hydraulic selector with separate levers for the bomb doors (10), undercarriage (11) and flaps (12). Beneath them is the aileron trim wheel (13) and the windscreen de-icing pump control (14). The control column yoke is in the centre (15) with the brake lever in line with the yoke's right arm (16). On the port side of the cockpit wall is the engine control box with the throttle levers (17) mounted at the top, propeller pitch controls (18) on the side, mixture control lever at the rear (19) plus the supercharger gear change switch on the side (20). The cold air intake control (21) is on the cockpit wall with the pilot's bomb release button (22) above and behind.

47

COCKPIT DEVELOPMENT

The cockpit canopy on single-stage Merlin Mosquito bomber variants differed little throughout the type's development.

Above: The cockpit canopy of the first prototype, W4050, photographed on 12 February 1941. The 'tear drop' shaped observation blisters (1) on the canopy side panels were a distinctive feature of bomber and photographic reconnaissance Mosquitoes until pressurised variants were introduced. Note that the direction vision panels (2) on W4050 originally hinged forward, obstructing the view through the windscreen; they were subsequently modified to hinge rearwards and to the side.

Upper right: With the canopy escape hatch removed, 105 Squadron's Commanding Officer, Wing Commander John Wooldridge, poses on the cockpit of a B.IV Series II at Marham. On production B. IVs the 'tear drop' shaped observation blisters were slightly smaller in size to those of W4050. Clearly visible in this photo is the DF loop (3) plus the two tubes (4) carrying the rudder trim cables from the canopy upper frame.

Below right: The first Canadian built Mosquitoes to reach the UK were not equipped with canopy observation blisters, these subsequently being added when the aircraft were prepared for service by 13 Maintenance Unit at Henlow. This is presentation B.XX KB162 'NEW GLASGOW'. Note the windscreen de-icing jet nozzle on the nose (5).

Upper left: The severely damaged rudder of 139 Squadron B.IV DZ597 'XD-L' following a collision with DZ423 'XD-K'. Both aircraft were returning from a raid Munich on 8 October 1943. Note the severed rudder trim tab connecting rod (A) plus the GEE whip aerial (B). The OBOE equipped Mosquitoes of 109 and 105 Squadrons operated with heavy bombers against special targets. However, 139 Squadron's aircraft - with G-H and (later on) H2S installed in the nose - would normally lead 8 Group's 'Light night Striking Force' (LNSF) Mosquitoes, Berlin being a regular target.

Lower left: Atmospheric photo of 139 Squadron B.IV Series II DZ519 'XD-U' running up on an unidentified Eight Air Force aerodrome. Returning from a raid on Berlin during the night of 20 October 1943, DZ519 was abandoned over Holland following the failure of all Gyro instruments plus both engines. Note the unshrouded exhausts.

Upper right: Photographed at Marham, this is an early OBOE equipped B.IV Series II of 109 Squadron, in this case DK331 'HS-D'. DK331 was regularly flown by Wg Cdr 'Hal' Bufton (second from the left) who played a crucial role in realising the installation of OBOE in Mosquitoes. Following flak damage incurred during its 103rd operation, DK331 was written off in April 1944 after crash landing at Little Staughton. As an early OBOE Mosquito, DK331 has yet to have its nose Perspex painted over. Note the windscreen de-icing jet fairing forward of the cockpit (C).

49

Main photo: Sporting their Night under surface finish, a brace of 627 Squadron B.IV Series II's cruise over a Cambridgeshire cloudscape. The squadron carried out several daylight operations, perhaps the most famous being an attack on the Gestapo Headquarters in Oslo on 31 December 1944.

Inset: Viewed from the port nose window of a 627 Squadron Mosquito, this is the squadron's 'A' Flight dispersal at Oakington in March 1944. The B.IV Series II in the centre is DZ353 'AZ-B' (see P.27), exhaust stubs having replaced the shrouds fitted during its 105 Squadron days.

627 Squadron ground crews conduct a Daily Inspection ('DI") on B.IV Series II DZ615 'AZ-Y'. Among the penultimate production batch of B. IV's, DZ615 originally served with 139 Squadron. DZ615 wears the standard Mosquito bomber scheme of Dark Green and Ocean Grey upper surfaces with Medium Sea Grey under surfaces. The 627 Squadron code letters 'AZ' are applied over a roughly applied patch of Ocean Grey, the latter concealing DZ615's former 139 Squadron codes. The inscription on the inside of the crew entrance hatch reads 'BEWARE OF AIRSCREWS' (1). Note the blanking plate over the trailing aerial tube exit (2) plus the fire extinguisher on the starboard engine bulkhead (3). The square shaped frame above the entry hatch window is thought to be connected with the drift sight (4).

627 Squadron aircrew Plt Off J.G.D. Platts (right) and navigator C.G. Thompson (RCAF) pose with B.IV Series II DZ521 'AZ-M' at Woodhall Spa. Displaying an impressive 91 mission tally, this veteran Mosquito previously served with 105 and 139 Squadrons before joining 627 in April 1944. DZ521 was eventually lost on 27 September 1944 when it crashed near Kings Lynn while returning from a raid on Karlsruhe. The streamlined fairing on the lower cowling (A) provided space for the connection between the lower section of the coolant header tank and the pipe running to the circulating pump. Note the ground crew's 'flag' marker on the Air Speed Indicator Static Head (B).

MOSQUITO B.IV SERIES II DZ521, AZ-M, 627 SQUADRON, SUMMER 1944

MODELLER'S NOTES

Aircraft:
Late production B.IV Series II.
Long undercarriage nacelles extending beyond wing trailing edge.
'No.2 Tailplane' 20ft 9in in span.
Metal covered elevators.
Five exhaust stubs on engine inboard and outboard sides.
Longitudinal stiffening strake on starboard side of fuselage above rear access hatch.
'Marstrand' double ridged, anti-shimmy, tail wheel tyre.
'Tear Drop' observation blisters on canopy side panels.
Single Navigation light on wingtip leading edges.
RESIN formation lights on wingtip trailing edges, in line with ailerons.
Ice guards on lower cowling carburettor air intakes.
No fixed aerial mast fitted.
GEE whip aerial extending from rear of cockpit canopy.
Fairing fitted to windscreen de-icing jet nozzle on nose upper surface.
Trailing aerial tube beneath nose.
Single lamp (Navigation) mounted on upper extremity of tail cone.
Single disc-brakes (with slotted mainwheel hubs on port outer, and starboard inner, respectively).
Inconel heat resistant panel inserts on engine side cowlings, aft of exhaust stubs.
91 yellow painted bomb symbol markings on port side of nose, the two upper rows are positioned between artwork of a figure playing the bag pipes.

Above: 627 Squadron B.IV Series II DZ525 'AZ-S' (later recoded 'AZ-B') photographed on the unit's B Flight dispersal at Woodhall Spa. Constructed at Hatfield in March 1943, DZ525 enjoyed a long career, serving with 109, 692 and 627 Squadrons before being Struck Off Charge in September 1945.

Right: View from the navigator's position of a 627 Squadron Mosquito B.IV Series II showing the bomb sight (1), forward navigation lamp (2), engine feathering buttons (3), artificial horizon (4), rate of climb and descent indicator (5) plus the turn and slip indicator (6). The hydraulic selector is mid-left with actuation levers for the bomb doors (7), undercarriage (8) and flaps; directly below that is the aileron trim wheel and position indicator (9). Although equipped with a bomb sight, 627 Squadron's Mosquitoes - in accordance with their low-level visual marking techniques - had the bomb release button positioned on the right-hand yoke of the pilot's control column wheel.

54

Right: Photographed at Hatfield on 18 May 1944 the identity of this B.IV Series II is believed to be DZ355 'XD-Q' of 139 Squadron. Note the bomb tally recording seventy-six operations including nineteen to Berlin. DZ355 entered service with 105 Squadron in October 1942 before passing to 139 Squadron in July 1943. It was fitted with G-H and H2S early in 1944 and amassed a total of 104 operational sorties before passing to 1655 Mosquito Training Unit (MTU) by the end of the year. Note the damage repair patch on the starboard inner cowling (1) plus the GEE whip aerial extending aft of the canopy (2). The significance of the name 'Sir Peter' is presently unknown.

Left: Fg Off J.R. Goodman (right) and his navigator Fg Off A.J.L. Hickox in front of their 627 Squadron B.IV Series II DZ484 'AZ-G' at Oakington. DZ484 features the Dark Green and Ocean Grey upper surface camouflage with Night under surface finish extending up the fuselage sides. DZ484 was regularly flown by Fg Off Goodman and went with him when both were posted to 1655 Mosquito Training Unit (MTU) in 1944.

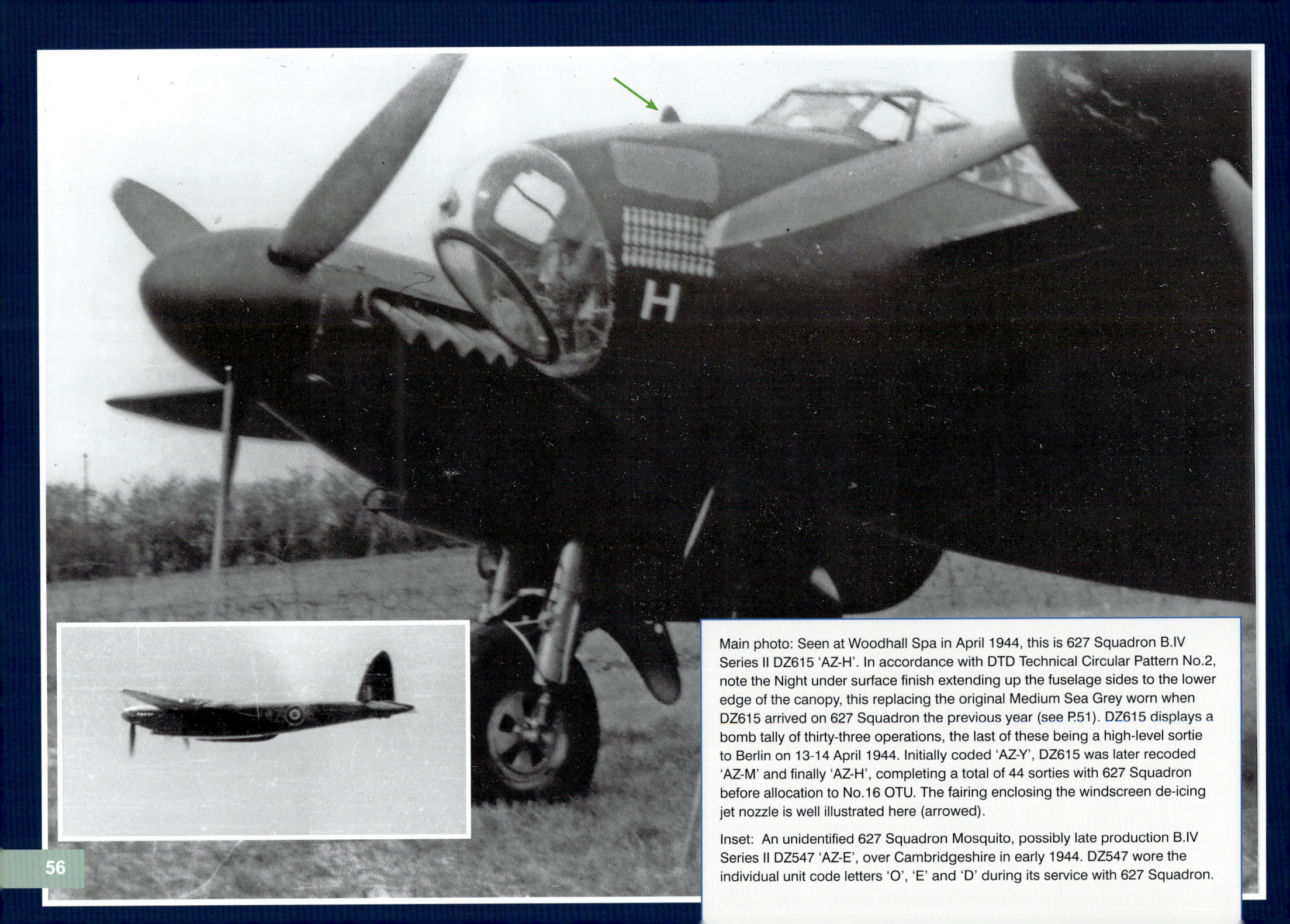

Main photo: Seen at Woodhall Spa in April 1944, this is 627 Squadron B.IV Series II DZ615 'AZ-H'. In accordance with DTD Technical Circular Pattern No.2, note the Night under surface finish extending up the fuselage sides to the lower edge of the canopy, this replacing the original Medium Sea Grey worn when DZ615 arrived on 627 Squadron the previous year (see P.51). DZ615 displays a bomb tally of thirty-three operations, the last of these being a high-level sortie to Berlin on 13-14 April 1944. Initially coded 'AZ-Y', DZ615 was later recoded 'AZ-M' and finally 'AZ-H', completing a total of 44 sorties with 627 Squadron before allocation to No.16 OTU. The fairing enclosing the windscreen de-icing jet nozzle is well illustrated here (arrowed).

Inset: An unidentified 627 Squadron Mosquito, possibly late production B.IV Series II DZ547 'AZ-E', over Cambridgeshire in early 1944. DZ547 wore the individual unit code letters 'O', 'E' and 'D' during its service with 627 Squadron.

MOSQUITO B.IV SERIES II DZ615, AZ-H, 627 SQUADRON, APRIL 1944

MODELLER'S NOTES

Aircraft:

Late production B.IV Series II.
Long undercarriage nacelles extending beyond wing trailing edge.
'No.2 Tailplane' 20ft 9in in span.
Metal covered elevators.
Five exhaust stubs on engine inboard and outboard sides.
Longitudinal stiffening strake on starboard side of fuselage above rear access hatch.
'Marstrand' double ridged, anti-shimmy, tail wheel tyre.
'Tear Drop' observation blisters on canopy side panels.
Single Navigation light on wingtip leading edge.
RESIN formation lights on wingtip trailing edges, in line with ailerons.
Ice guards on lower cowling carburettor air intakes.
No fixed aerial mast.
GEE whip aerial extending from rear of cockpit canopy.
Fairing fitted to windscreen de-icing jet nozzle on nose upper surface.
Trailing aerial tube beneath nose.
Single lamp (Navigation) mounted on upper extremity of tail cone.
Single disc-brakes (with slotted mainwheel hubs on port outer, and starboard inner, respectively).
Inconel heat resistant panel inserts on engine side cowlings, aft of exhaust stubs.

Below: Brand new B.IV Series II DZ599 awaiting an acceptance test flight at Hatfield in May 1943. By this time the formation keeping light on Mosquito wingtips (see P.8) had been replaced by RESIN (Restricted Intensity) Lamps located on the wingtip trailing edge, directly in line with the outboard edge of the aileron (A). Like all B. IV's, DZ599 also features single disc-brakes (with slotted mainwheel hubs on port outer, and starboard inner, respectively) (B). Converted to carry the 4000lb bomb, DZ599 initially served with 692 Squadron but passed to 627 Squadron in June 1944. As 'AZ-F', DZ599 flew thirty-five operations with 627 until it ditched off the East Frisian Islands on the night of 27 March 1945.

Right: A rare image featuring B. IV's inside the Mosquito Servicing Section (MSS) Flight hangar at RAF Upwood. Conceived by 8 Group Engineering Officer Group Captain Sarsby, the MSS Flight helped maintain the general high level of servicibility of all 8 Group Pathfinder Force Mosquitoes. In addition to conducting Major Servicing, the MSS continued the development of new Marks of OBOE such as Mk. 2, Mk. 3 and multi-channel. Note the 109 Squadron aircraft on the left.

CARRYING THE COOKIE

Main photo: In April 1943 the Ministry of Aircraft Production (MAP) instructed de Havilland's to modify a single B.IV Series II to carry the 4000lb 'Cookie' blast bomb. The trial installation was undertaken on DZ594 seen here at Hatfield on 29 November 1943. The 'Cookie' was suspended from a hook attached to spruce beams running between the front and rear spars of the wing, the bomb doors also being enlarged to project beneath the fuselage line, presenting a somewhat 'pregnant' appearance. Note the two drain plugs for the starboard cabin heater unit, visible beneath the inboard section of the radiator housing (A).

Inset right: Another view of DZ594 showing the forward fairing for the enlarged bomb bay doors (arrowed). Note the 'needle' blade propellers and shrouded exhausts.

Main photo: Lovely photograph of DZ594/G during trials at A&AEE Boscombe Down. DZ594's 4000lb bomb conversion took only seven weeks, the first flight taking place in July 1943. The aft fairing for the enlarged bomb bay doors is well illustrated here (1). Unique to DZ594, note the 'fluted' extensions to the oil drain outlets on the lower cowlings (2). Silver dope has been applied to the sealing strip between the rear fuselage and tailplane, visible just aft of the serial number (3).

Right: DZ594 was equipped with metal elevators, the port unit appears to be a new replacement in this photograph. While carrying the 4000lb bomb DZ594 proved divergently unstable, this was partly overcome by fitting enlarged elevator horn balances, the latter becoming standard on all B. IVs subsequently modified to accommodate the 'Cookie'.

Above: Looking aft along the port side of DZ594's bomb bay. Note the rear bracing arch bolted to the upper and lower sections of the fuselage side panel (1) plus the handle for the aft bomb winch (2).

Above right: The starboard mid-fuselage of DZ594 clearly showing the 'swollen' bomb bay doors plus their streamlined aft fairing. Note the reinforcing strap over the fuselage bulkhead three (3).

Lower right: Viewed immediately forward of fuselage bulkhead two, this is DZ594's bomb bay looking aft. Clearly visible are the forward (4) and rear (5) bomb bay bracing arches plus the rear crutches (6) for carriage of the 4000lb 'Cookie' (the forward crutches are not visible here). At middle top is the front bomb winch (7) with the two 68-gallon centre section fuel tanks on either side (5).

Lower left: The rear of DZ594's bomb bay showing the extended lower profile of fuselage bulkhead four (9), necessary to align with the enlarged bomb bay doors.

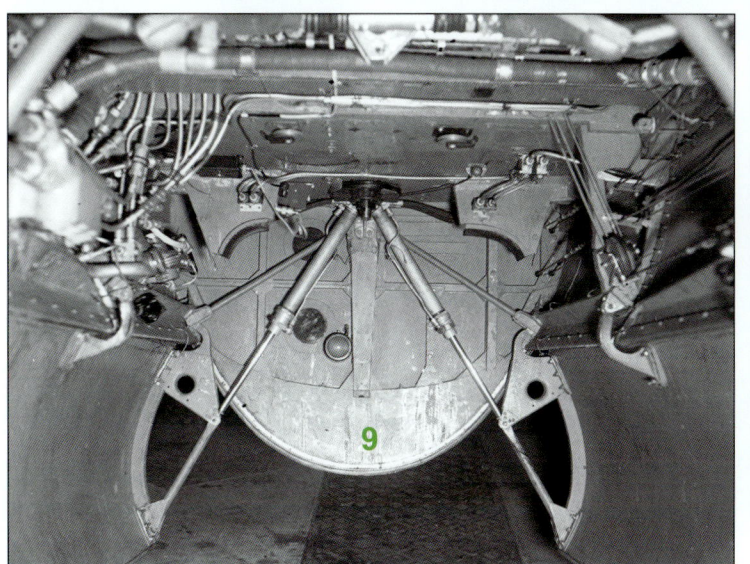

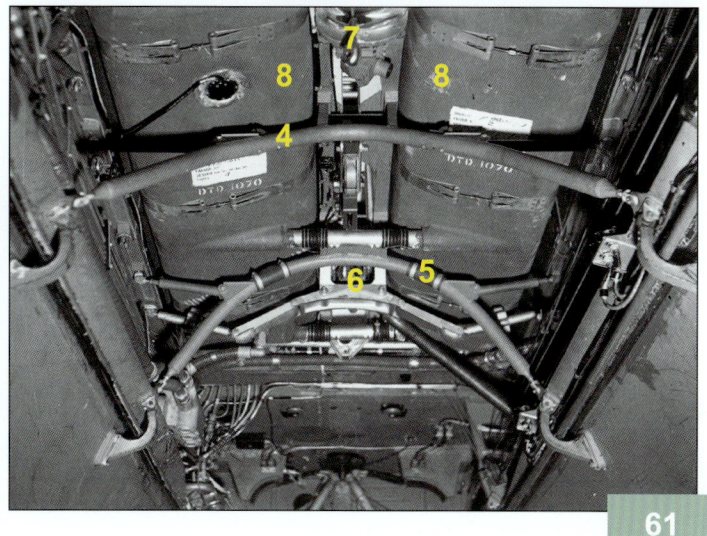

Main Photo: At Graveley in 1944, aircrew of 692 Squadron hitch a lift aboard a 4000lb 'Cookie' destined for one of the unit's Mosquitoes. The aircraft behind them is DZ637 'P3-C' which was converted to carry the 'Cookie' during the summer of 1944. Initially assigned to 627 Squadron, DZ637 passed to 692 Squadron two weeks later, completing forty-six operations before reallocation to 627 Squadron in July 1944. As 'AZ-X' DZ637 was shot down in February 1945 during a raid on Steigen. Note the Night under surface finish which extends up the fuselage sides and completely covers the fin and rudder. The upper surfaces are finished in Ocean Grey and Dark Green with the squadron code letters in red.

Upper right: In total twenty-seven B.IV Series II Mosquitoes were converted to carry the 4000lb bomb, this is DZ632 'AZ-C' of 627 Squadron seen at Oakington in March 1944. Note the enlarged horn balance on the starboard elevator (arrowed). Production conversions of 4000lb bomb carrying B. IVs were known as 'B.IV Series II Specials'.

692 Squadron armourers winch a 4000lb 'Cookie' aboard DZ637 'P3-C' at Graveley. Two special winches were provided for this task, both permanently attached to the wing centre section. The winch handles (the forward winch is seen here at (1)) engaged with a universal coupling, the rear winch featuring an adjustable cable guide enabling the bomb to be offered up straight to the release gear. To prevent overloading of the winches and hoisting cables, a friction device was incorporated in both winch handles at their point of attachment to the winch shaft.

THE CANADIAN B.XX AND B.25

Main photo: In the hands of de Havilland Canada Chief Test Pilot Ralph Spradbrow, the first Canadian built Mosquito, B.VII KB300, makes its maiden flight on 24 September 1942. The flight took place just over a year from receipt of the first batch of drawings from Britain. Accompanying Ralph Spradbrow on this inaugural flight was de Havilland Hatfield flight shed engineer, Pepe Burrell.

Inset right: A pre-first flight photograph of KB300 undergoing engine runs at the de Havilland Canada Downsview plant in September 1942. The Canadian B.VII was based upon the projected British B.V but powered by American built Packard Merlin 31 engines. KB300 looks magnificent in silver dope finish with black spinners.

Main photo: A line-up of 36 OTU Mosquito B. XX's, plus a single T.III, at Greenwood, Nova Scotia, in February 1944. Nearest the camera is B.XX KB179.

Right: Twenty-five Mosquito B.VII's were constructed in Canada, KB304 being the fifth example. Looking very much like an early B.IV Series II, note the shrouded exhausts, Sky rear fuselage band and spinners plus the single disc-brakes (with slotted mainwheel hubs on port outer, and starboard inner, respectively).

Inset left: The RAF's first five Canadian built Mosquitoes lined up for a christening ceremony at Downsview. All B. XX's, they were named after Canadian cities with the highest sales record in a Victory Bonds drive. The individual aircraft were (bottom to top): KB161 'Vancouver'; KB329 'Moose Jaw'; KB160 'Saskatoon': KB328 'Acton' and KB162 'New Glasgow'. Although all are equipped with 'saxophone' exhaust manifolds within flame damping shrouds, these would be replaced by exhaust stubs prior to delivery.

Main photo: KB160 'Saskatoon' and KB329 'Moose Jaw' photographed at Prestwick following their trans-Atlantic delivery flights in August 1943. Note the opened access door to KB160's coolant header tank filler cap (arrowed).

66

Upper Left: KB328 'Acton' was the first of the Canadian B. XX's to reach the UK, seen here with a reception party at Hatfield on 12 August 1943. Standing fifth from the left (with his back to the camera) is the Mosquito's Chief Designer, Ronald Bishop (A).

Upper right: KB328 with its transatlantic delivery crew (right to left), Plt Off Uren (pilot) and Flg Off R.C. Bevington (navigator). Like all early B. XX's, KB328 is not equipped with 'tear drop' shaped observation blisters on the canopy side panels.

Right: Also pictured at Hatfield on 12 August 1943 is KB162 'New Glasgow', the second B.XX to reach the UK. KB162 wears the Fighter Command special recognition markings of Sky rear fuselage band, Sky spinners plus yellow striped wing leading edges. Note the metal 50-gallon underwing drop tanks, twin disc brake units on the main wheel hubs plus the lack of a fairing around the windscreen de-icing jet nozzle (B).

Another photograph of B.XX KB162, this time being bombed-up at Upwood in 1944 while serving with 139 squadron as 'XD-J'. 139 Squadron pioneered the operational use of Canadian built Mosquitoes, B.XX KB161 'XD-H' making the type's first sortie on 2 December 1943. KB162 has changed considerably since its arrival in the UK (see P.67), the perspex nose having been replaced by a new 'Triplex' radome housing H2S radar. Additionally, 'tear drop' observation blisters have now been installed on the canopy side panels and the bomb bay forward camera ports painted over. KB162's original yellow striped wing leading edge markings have also been removed along with the Sky rear fuselage band and Sky spinners; the latter now refinished in Night. On 14 October 1944 KB162 crashed shortly after take-off from Warboys. The inscription immediately forward and above the 'NEW GLASGOW' titling reads 'SPOT ON".

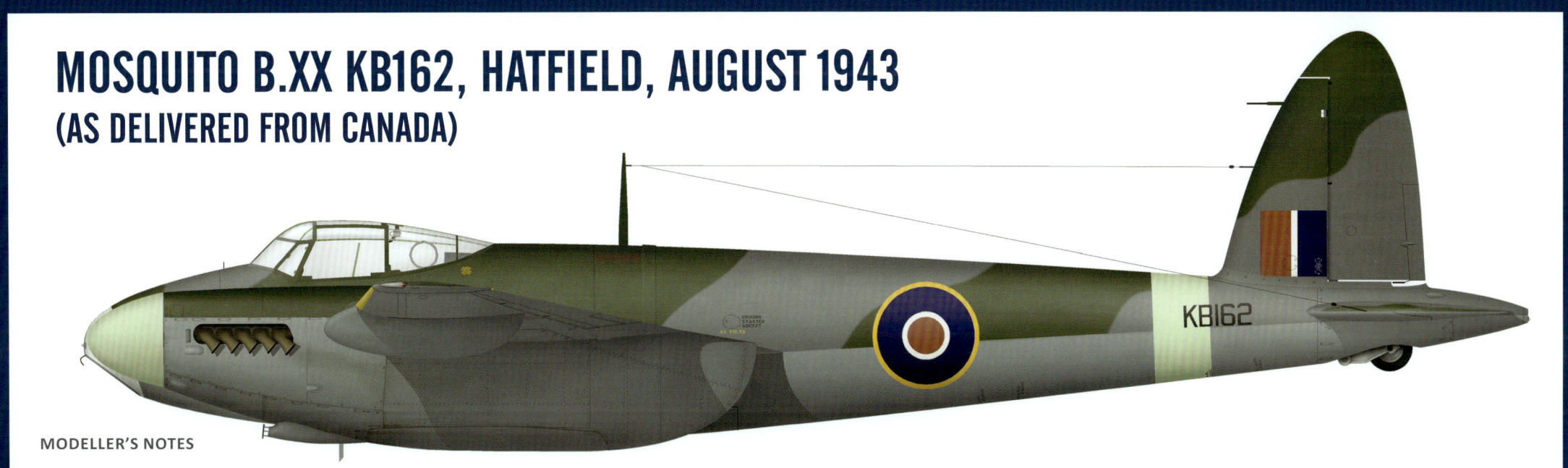

MOSQUITO B.XX KB162, HATFIELD, AUGUST 1943
(AS DELIVERED FROM CANADA)

MODELLER'S NOTES

Aircraft:
Early production B.XX.
Long undercarriage nacelles extending beyond wing trailing edge.
'No.2 Tailplane' 20ft 9in in span.
Fabric covered elevators.
Five exhaust stubs on engine inboard and outboard sides.
Longitudinal stiffening strake on starboard side of fuselage above rear access hatch.
'Marstrand' double ridged, anti-shimmy, tail wheel tyre.
'Tear Drop' observation blisters not fitted.
Single Navigation light on wingtip leading edge.
RESIN formation light on wingtip trailing edge in line with aileron.
Ice guards on lower cowling carburettor air intakes.
Fixed aerial mast with Bakelite mounting ring surround.
No fairing fitted to windscreen de-icing jet nozzle on nose upper surface.
Trailing aerial tube beneath nose.
Single lamp (Navigation) mounted on lower extremity of tail cone.
Metal fifty-gallon underwing drop tanks.
Yellow wing leading edge stripes within 3 ft of the engine nacelle outboard side. Width of stripe 7in at the inboard end tapering to 3 in wide at the wingtip. Centreline of the stripe is on the centreline of the wing leading edge.

Discussion points:
Engine cowling side panels have chromium nickel aft sections in place of the Inconel heat resistant inserts featured on British built Mosquitoes. On KB162 these chromium nickel panels were finished in Medium Sea Grey, along with the remainder of the side cowlings.

70

Opposite page: The cockpit of a B.XX photographed on the de Havilland Canada Downsview production line. Essentially similar in layout to the British built B.IV Series II, the principal external difference is the use of North American instrumentation in place of British manufactured items. Note the blind flying panel in its 'crackle' paint finish (1); the engine instrumentation on the left-hand side (2); plus, the engine control box on the port cockpit wall with the throttle levers mounted at the top (3); propeller pitch controls on the side (4); and the supercharger gear change switch at the rear (5). Beneath the blind flying panel are the engine starter (6) and booster coil push buttons (7); the group of four magneto switches (8); the flap position indicator (9); and the brake pressure gauge (10). To the right of the flap indicator is the hydraulic selector with separate levers for the bomb doors (11); undercarriage (12); and flaps (13). Beneath these is the aileron trim wheel (14); and the windscreen de-icing pump control (15). The control column yoke is lower left (16) with the brake lever in line with the yoke's right arm (17). The landing light selector switches are visible at (18).

Upper right: With its canopy escape hatch removed, this is the cockpit of a B.XX photographed at Hatfield in October 1943. Note the internal cockpit door (with the drift sight opening at the rear) folded upwards and secured in position (1); the navigators chart table folded against the cockpit wall (2); the stowage position for the SYKO deciphering equipment in the nose (3) plus the door to the entrance ladder stowage compartment beneath the floor (4). On the starboard side of the cockpit is Junction Box B housing the fuel contents gauges (5); IFF detonator buttons (6); IFF switch (7); navigation headlamp switch (8) plus the downward identification lamps switch (9).

Lower right: Close-up of the port Packard Merlin 31 on a B.XX showing the two rearmost exhaust stubs 'Siamesed' into one. To increase the longevity of exhaust stubs considerable research and development was undertaken to find the most suitable material. This resulted in the use of Inconel exhaust stubs on Canadian Mosquitoes, these demonstrating up to 300% longer life compared to the British designed stainless-steel stubs.

71

Right: B.XX KB125, the seventy-fifth Canadian built Mosquito, shows evidence of a major oil leak from the port engine. Applied to all but the initial Canadian built bombers, this is a good illustration of the Canadian practice of extending the upper surface camouflage down the forward panel of the engine side cowlings (1). In comparison to the earlier B.VII (plus the British B. IV's), note the twin-disc brake units on the mainwheel hubs.

Below: The tail of KB125 showing the navigation lamp positioned on the lower extremity of the tail cone (2) plus further evidence of the port engine oil leak, this time around the lower fuselage beneath the stiffening strake (3). KB125 went on to serve with 139 Squadron and 16 OTU, ending its days when the undercarriage collapsed at Barford St. John on 20 March 1945.

Opposite page: The fifth batch of B. XX's on the Downsview production line in April 1944. On the middle left (A) is KB251, this aircraft remained in Canada throughout its career, serving in the training role with 31 OTU, and later 7 OTU, of the RCAF. Some 670 Mosquito bombers were manufactured in Canada out of a ground total of 1133 aircraft of various marques. During the program, the design and manufacture of tools, jigs and fixtures was a major problem. Tool drawings and data received from the UK fell far short of meeting total tool drawing requirements. An estimated 2000 British tool drawings were received but many were unusable, having to be revised to conform with American processing standards. Note the protective mats on the wing upper surfaces (B) plus the port radiator access panel behind the workers in the foreground (C).

73

Below: Late production B.XX KB352 never saw RAF squadron service, being employed on IFF and radio compass trials at A&AEE Boscombe Down. Note the unpainted chromium nickel (heat resistant) aft section of the engine side cowling (1) with its blister fairing covering the engine hand crank point (2). Canadian Mosquito side cowlings differed in construction to their British counterparts; the chromium nickel panel of Canadian aircraft replacing the small Inconel heat resistant 'square' of British side cowlings. The characteristic 'wavy' Dark Green camouflage demarcation of Canadian Mosquitoes is well illustrated here

Inset left: Canadian built B.XX KB233 on display at Hatfield following a record-breaking crossing of the Atlantic (coast to coast) from Labrador to Britain in 5 hours and 40 minutes. Flown by Wing Commander John Wooldridge (former Commanding Officer of 105 Squadron), and navigated by Flying Officer C.J. Bown, the flight took place on 13 May 1944.

Below: B.25 KB669 photographed at 13 MU Henlow in April 1945. The third and final production Canadian bomber variant, the B.25 was developed from the B.XX but featured the more powerful Packard Merlin 225 engines. Note KB669's 'paddle' blade propellers and 100-gallon underwing drop tanks. Also noteworthy is the external locking plate on the undercarriage doors (A) which formed part of Mod 499 introduced in March 1944. Mod 499 provided a positive up-lock for the undercarriage doors to prevent them opening too far in flight and - more importantly - to stop the doors being torn off in the slipstream should a door cable break. It incorporated an additional tube on the undercarriage leg fenders (B), this engaging with locks positioned on the inside of the undercarriage doors. Due to differences in Canadian nacelle and undercarriage door lines, considerable work was necessary to adapt Mod 499 for Canadian Mosquito production. The Type 312 aerial beneath the nose (C) is believed to be for the Type 3624 transmitter-receiver.

Inset right: Taken at Hatfield in January 1945, this is a staged photo depicting loading of a 1000lb target indicator bomb aboard a snow-covered B.XX, possibly KB226.

Brand new B.25's in Canada awaiting delivery to the UK. The aircraft in the centre is KB660 which arrived in the UK during early 1945, passing to the Admiralty on 3 August the same year. In January 1946 KB660 was allocated to 733 Squadron, Fleet Air Arm, at Trinconmalee in Ceylon. Note the unpainted chromium nickel aft section of the engine side cowling (1). One de Havilland representative in the UK reported that 'Canadian Mosquitoes are popular and reported to be "considerably faster" than English built, swing less and have more stability at height: the last two points are probably incorrect.' KB660 was sold as scrap in February 1946.

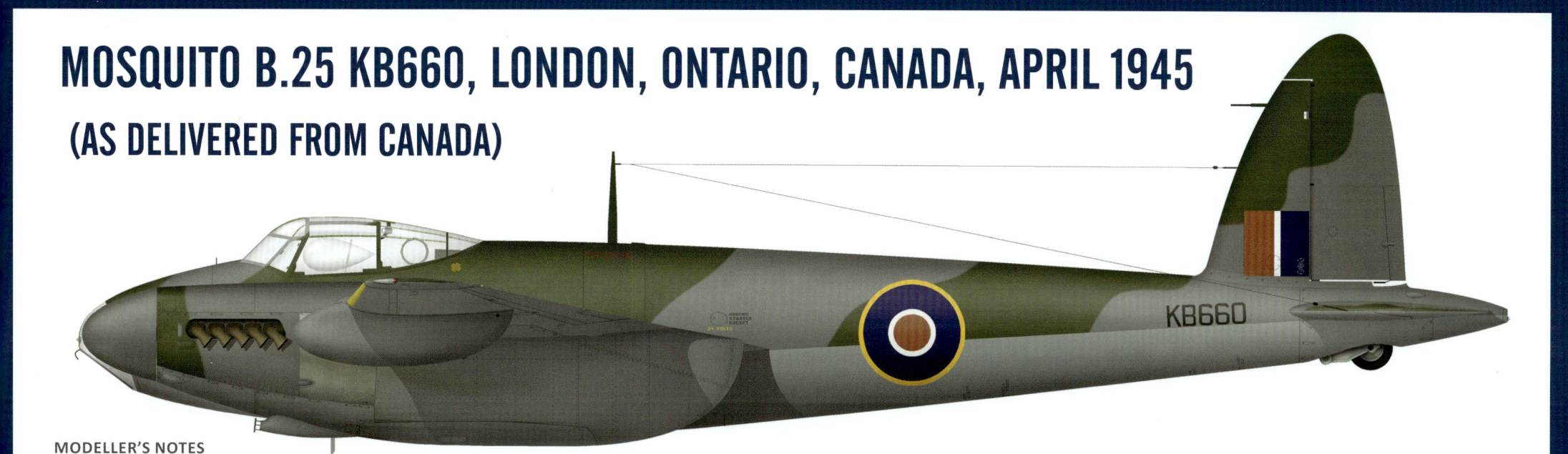

MOSQUITO B.25 KB660, LONDON, ONTARIO, CANADA, APRIL 1945
(AS DELIVERED FROM CANADA)

MODELLER'S NOTES

Aircraft:
Mid production B.25.
Long undercarriage nacelles extending beyond wing trailing edge.
'No.2 Tailplane' 20ft 9in in span.
Metal covered elevators.
Five exhaust stubs on engine inboard and outboard sides.
Longitudinal stiffening strake on starboard side of fuselage above rear access hatch.
'Marstrand' double ridged, anti-shimmy, tail wheel tyre.
'Tear Drop' observation blisters on canopy side panels.
Single Navigation light on wingtip leading edge.
RESIN formation light on wingtip trailing edges in line with aileron.
Ice guards on lower cowling carburettor air intakes.
Fixed aerial mast with Bakelite mounting ring surround.
No fairing fitted to windscreen de-icing jet nozzle on nose upper surface.
Trailing aerial tube beneath nose.
Single lamp (Navigation) mounted on lower extremity of tail cone.
100 gallon underwing drop tanks.
Mod 499 locking plates on exterior of undercarriage doors.

Discussion points:
Engine cowling side panels feature chromium nickel aft sections in place of the Inconel heat resistant inserts featured on British built Mosquitoes. On KB660 these chromium nickel sections were left in natural metal finish, however the side cowling forward sections were camouflaged in Ocean Grey and Dark Green

Below: On 17 April 1945 B.25 KA970 was on the last leg of its trans-Atlantic delivery flight from Canada. Seventy-five miles out from Prestwick, while descending from 19,000ft, the crew heard a loud explosion which knocked the pilot's feet from the rudder pedals. The starboard engine then began to lose power, so the propeller was feathered as the aircraft continued on to the Scottish coast. All attempts to lower the undercarriage by hand pump failed, KA970 subsequently making a belly landing on the Prestwick runway. It transpired that a regulator had frozen causing an air bottle to explode, the starboard side of the fuselage being severely damaged in the process. Note the missing escape hatch on top of the canopy, the crew exiting through this point as the access hatch under the nose was blocked in the belly landing.

Upper left: KA970's fuselage at Hatfield showing the damage caused by the air bottle explosion, the starboard fuselage skin blown away over an area approximately seven feet by two. Note the damage to bulkhead five which has been torn in half (arrowed), bulkheads three and four (not visible here) having been severed for around twelve feet of their circumference. Additionally, the hydraulic oil tank was destroyed and bulkhead 6 distorted.

Right: B.25 KB529 photographed en-route to the UK in early 1945. KB529 was allocated to 163 Squadron based at RAF Wyton. On 22 April 1945 it was shot down by flak during a raid on Kiel. Note the 100-gallon underwing drop tanks, the latter necessary to increase range during the transatlantic delivery flights. In order to produce these tanks in Canada it was necessary to 'productionise' the original British design.

Left: Converted from B.25 KB471, the one-off Mosquito 'B.23' (two-stage Merlin 69's) conversion shows off its enlarged bomb bay doors to accommodate the 4000lb 'Cookie' (see P.59). Five other B.25's were modified to carry the 4000lb bomb, namely KB409, KB416, KB490, KB561 and KB625. This also illustrates the wavy 'meandering' Dark Green camouflage demarcation applied to Canadian Mosquitoes. The second Mosquito Bombers volume of this series will cover KB471 in more detail.

Early production B.XX KB144 'F' was retained in Canada for the training of Mosquito aircrews. It is seen here while on the strength 36 OTU's 'C' Flight at Greenwood, Nova Scotia. in June 1944. Like many of the early B. XX's KB144 is finished in the short-lived (on British Mosquito bombers) Day Fighter Scheme of Sky rear fuselage band, Sky spinners plus yellow striped wing leading edges. Note the Inconel rear panel of the port engine side cowling plus the twin-disc brake hubs. KB144 is not equipped with the 'tear drop' shaped observation blisters on the canopy side panels. Later allocated to No.7 OTU RCAF, KB144 was written off after crashing during a training flight on 22 May 1945.